Better Homes and Gardens®

DO·IT·YOURSELF

DECKS · PATIOS
FENCES · WALKS

Excerpted from Better Homes and Gardens®
Complete Guide to Home Repair, Maintenance, and Improvement
© Copyright 1989 by Meredith Corporation, Des Moines, Iowa.
All Rights Reserved. Printed in the United States of America.
First Edition. First Printing.
ISBN: 0-696-01869-1

INTRODUCTION

Some of today's most rewarding home fix-ups aren't even in the home. Improvements *outside* your home—outdoor living areas, fences, walks, garden walls, and other landscape enhancers—will increase your home's comfort and beauty now. And, they'll raise its value when you're ready to sell.

Better Homes and Gardens® *Do-It-Yourself Decks, Patios, Fences, and Walks* shows you, step by step, how to add new outdoor amenities and how to solve problems with the ones you already enjoy. With hundreds of concise, easy-to-follow illustrations, this book gives you the information and the confidence you need to make your yard and outdoor living areas better than ever.

BETTER HOMES AND GARDENS® BOOKS
Editor: Gerald M. Knox
Art Director: Ernest Shelton
Managing Editor: David A. Kirchner
Editorial Project Managers: Liz Anderson, James D. Blume,
    Marsha Jahns, Jennifer Speer Ramundt, Angela Renkoski

Do-It-Yourself Decks, Patios, Fences, and Walks
Editors: Gayle Goodson Butler and James A. Hufnagel
Editorial Project Manager: Liz Anderson
Electronic Text Processor: Paula Forest

Complete Guide to Home Repair, Maintenance, and Improvement
Project Editors: Larry Clayton, Noel Seney
Research and Writing: James A. Hufnagel
Graphic Designer: Richard Lewis
Illustrations: Graphic Center

CONTENTS

PATIOS AND DECKS

Sooner or later, weather takes its toll on all outdoor living areas—even super-tough concrete patios. The following pages show how to undo the damage and prevent its recurrence.

But the problem at most homes is that there isn't enough outdoor living space. So we've devoted the bulk of this section to telling how to lay a brick patio, how to pour a concrete slab, and how to get a sturdy deck off the ground.

ANATOMY OF A PATIO

Regardless of the patio's surface—usually *concrete, brick,* or *flagstone*—it usually rests on a *sand base.* Large expanses of concrete paving require *expansion strips* between them and other structures (house foundations, for example) and *control joints* to help keep any possible cracking in check. Concrete also usually requires *reinforcing mesh* or *rods* for strength and to prevent cracking. Brick and stone units "float" on the sand base or rest in a bed of mortar.

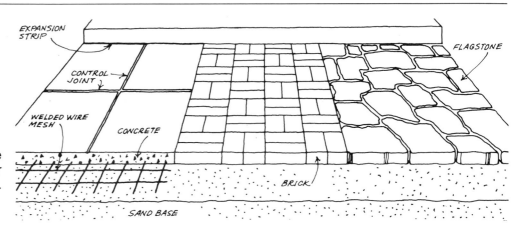

PATIO SURFACE STAIN REMOVAL GUIDE	
Type of Stain	**Remedy**
Food, grease, oil, lipstick	Mix dishwashing detergent in warm water. Work the mixture into the stain with a stiff scrub brush or broom. Don't skimp. Rinse with clean water. If this doesn't work, add ammonia to the detergent and water mixture, following the same rinsing procedures mentioned above. Or scrub well with mineral spirits.
Paint and candle wax	Remove all the paint or wax you can with a knife or a putty knife. Then scrub the area with metal-bristled brush and cold water. If this fails, apply mineral spirits to the area. If the stain is on concrete and these treatments don't work, try aluminum oxide abrasive or an abrasive brick.
Blood, coffee, juice, animal waste	Use dishwashing detergent in cold water. Remove the stain as soon as possible. Work with a stiff scrub brush or broom, and flood the area with the detergent mixture. Rinse with cold clean water.
Tar and heel marks	First try dishwashing detergent in warm water. If you're not successful, scour the area with a stiff-bristled brush and mineral spirits; don't use a scouring pad. If some residue remains, flood the area with mineral spirits and blot it up with a soft absorbent cloth. This may take several applications.
Efflorescence	Go over the area with a wire brush. This should remove the white stain, which is caused by salts in the masonry mixture. If this doesn't work, you can buy a commercial mixture that will remove the stain. It contains an acid, so be sure to wear gloves and safety glasses when using it.
Dirt and grime	Hose down the surface with water and scrub it with a stiff broom. If this doesn't do the job, mix dishwashing detergent or trisodium phosphate with warm water and go over the area with a stiff brush or broom.
Soot	Apply detergent and water. If this doesn't work, apply a mixture of one quart of muriatic acid and one quart of water. Wear gloves.

SOLVING PATIO PROBLEMS

Though it may hurt a bit to think of it this way, you repair a patio surface in much the same way a dentist fills a tooth: you clean away the old debris, prepare the cavity, and fill the void.

Don't, however, try to fill cavities in concrete with concrete; you won't get a good bond with the old surface. Instead, choose one of the commercial patching materials listed in the chart at right.

For stone and brick surfaces, you simply lever out the damaged unit, replace it with a new one, then pack around it with mortar. The illustrations below demonstrate the basic techniques. For more detailed information on repairing brick and stone, turn to pages 32 and 33.

CONCRETE PATCH SELECTOR		
Type	**Uses**	**Description/Mixing Instructions**
Latex patch Vinyl patch Epoxy patch	General-purpose repair jobs such as filling hairline cracks, small breaks and patches, and tuck-pointing. Latex and epoxy are best for patio surfaces.	Sold in powdered form with or without a liquid binder. Mix with the appropriate binder, usually a sticky white liquid, to a whipped-cream consistency.
Hydraulic cement	To plug water leaks in masonry walls and floor surfaces. This fast-drying formulation allows you to make the repair even while the water is leaking in.	Available in powdered form. Mix a small amount with water or a commercial binder, then work quickly.
Dry pre-mixed concrete	Wherever whole sections of concrete are being repaired.	Mix this product with water. The thicker the consistency, the faster it will set up.

Note: Mixing a synthetic binder with the patch material strengthens the repair and enables the patch to adhere more securely to the old surface.

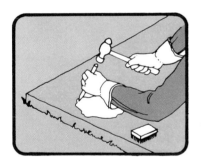

Chip away all cracked or crumbling material to solid concrete. Use a wire brush to clean any loose materials from crevices.

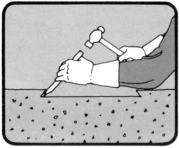

Undercut the edges of the damaged area to provide a "key," which will lock in the patch. Remove all loose materials.

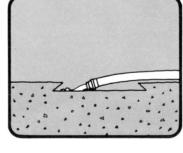

Dampen the area to be patched with water. Some patches call for priming the area with a water/portland cement mixture.

Tamp in the patching compound. Be sure to pack it firmly and try to mound it a bit to compensate for shrinkage.

When the patch begins to set up, smooth it with a trowel or straightedge. Cover the patch and let it cure for one week.

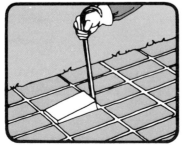

Remove damaged or misfitting stones or bricks. If the joints are mortar and have been damaged, use a latex or epoxy patch.

Level the cavity with sand or mortar. Tamp the area well before replacing the brick or stone, and tap it level. Then remortar.

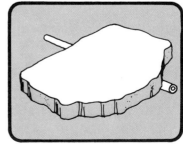

To move slabs or large flagstones, roll them on a length of pipe. And when lifting chunks of masonry, use your legs, not your back.

SOLVING DECK PROBLEMS

Especially if neglected, but even if well cared for, decks develop many of the same problems that plague porches—rot, plus a host of structural maladies.

Posts, beams, and joists are particularly prone to rot, as they're often near ground level and covered by decking. Steps and railings work loose through normal use, and finishes, no matter how tough, give way to weather.

A twice-yearly inspection is your best protection against letting your deck's condition decline. If problems develop, tend to them quickly. The chart below describes the course of action to follow for several common ailments.

ANATOMY OF A DECK

Like a porch, a deck is simple post-and-beam construction. The *decking* rests on *joists* and *beams,* which gain support from *posts* and *piers* or *footings.* And unless it's freestanding, the deck is tied to the house structure by a *ledger.* Joists sit on edge on the ledger. House joists also can be extended past the foundation wall (cantilevered) to form a support for the decking. On some decks, the posts extend up through the decking to function as part of the railing. On others, *balusters* fasten to joists or beams. A *cap rail* stabilizes and protects the other railing members.

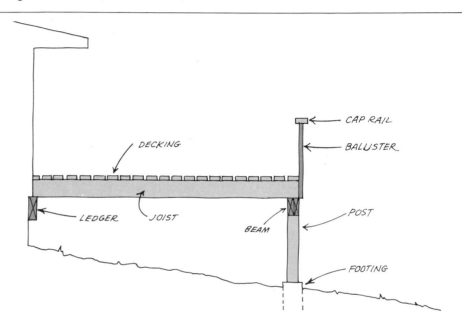

SOLVING DECK PROBLEMS			
Problem	**Solution**	**Problem**	**Solution**
Dirt, grime, grease, everyday stains	Wash the area thoroughly with mild household detergent. Rinse. See the stain removal chart on page 4.	Sap stains. finish bleed-throughs, finish failure	On unfinished wood, remove sap with mineral spirits. Prime bleeds and finish failures with clear shellac; refinish.
Mildew	Scrub the area with a mixture of water and household bleach, or use a commercial mildewcide.	Damaged decking and other deck components	Replacement parts are the best solution. See pages 17–21 for particulars on how decks are constructed (or reconstructed).

APPLYING STAINS AND PRESERVATIVES

As noted above, the finish protecting your deck will eventually succumb to the ravages of time and weather. Not even redwood, cedar, or pressure-treated wood will stand up forever.

Stains are by far the best dressings for a deck, so wherever possible use them. However, if your deck has been painted before, you'll have to settle for a fresh coat of paint after a thorough scraping.

If you opt for stain, be sure to ask for one formulated for exterior use, preferably one of the penetrating oil stains. These go beneath the wood's surface to give long-lasting protection and good looks. If you want the wood's grain to show, use a clear or semi-transparent stain. Or if you prefer a painted look, buy a solid-color stain. For painted surfaces, choose an exterior latex- or alkyd-base floor paint.

If you opt for a clear finish, choose an outdoor-grade varnish or polyurethane.

ADDING OUTDOOR LIVING AREAS

Your family's fair-weather life-style will get a big boost with the addition of a patio or deck. You'll find a well-planned outdoor living area can depressurize the interior spaces, just by adding alternative spots for cooking, eating, and relaxing.

Thoughtful up-front planning is well worth a little time; a long-range master plan will preclude later regrets. The four drawings below show excellent solutions for typical lots. Each has the big three ingredients you should include in your planning: an outdoor living area, outside storage facilities, and a service area. Add a play area if you have small children.

Start with the outdoor living facility first. The slope or flatness of your lot will help you decide whether to plan a deck or patio. Flat lots give you a complete choice from bricks-in-sand patios to an on-grade deck. If you have a slope to work around, you may find an elevated deck the only practical alternative.

Then study the area's relationship to the interior floor plan. You'll need access for convenience' sake, so take advantage of existing doors, or consider installing a sliding glass door. With these generalities in mind, next plan the location and size of the storage units you'll want.

The third step is to work out a spot for the service area. Make it large enough to handle garbage cans, a stack of firewood, potting benches, or whatever your family requires.

You may want to use graph paper and sketch in these things to scale, or you may find it easiest to stake out the areas on a trial-and-error basis. At this point you also should check for lot restrictions.

Many zoning regulations require outbuildings and decks to be a specified distance from your lot lines. Be sure you don't build on a part of your lot on which there's an easement—nor over an underground utility, such as a septic system.

All that's left in your planning is the privacy and screening you'll need. Consider the plantings you have and will add as well as fences you might want to build (see pages 24–30).

With your long-range goals established, you're ready to work out the exact size of your deck or patio and gather prices for the materials. And with the know-how that follows, doing it yourself will yield three very worthwhile results—convenience, comfort for years to come, and more money in your pocket.

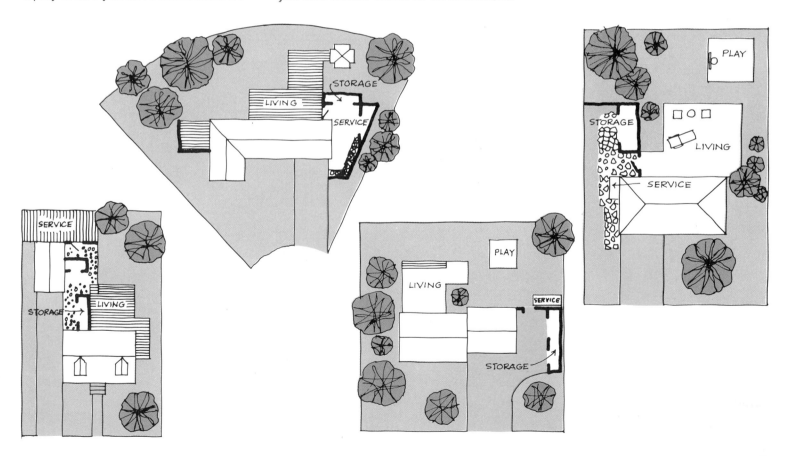

LAYING A PATIO IN SAND

If you've decided that you can't get along any longer without a patio, yet you don't really care for the look of concrete, why not consider laying bricks, flagstones, slate, paving blocks, or precast patio blocks in sand. The procedures involved are relatively simple, and you won't need many special tools—a mason's hammer, brick chisel, shovel, nail hammer, garden hose, broom, and a level will see you through.

In addition to the surfacing material of your choice, you'll also need a goodly amount of sand to serve as a base. The amount required for your project depends on the site, which should be fairly level. For a 10x20-foot patio, you'll need about 2.5 cubic yards of sand to provide a four-inch base; in a well-drained area, you could get by with a two-inch base—and only half as much sand.

The sketch below gives you a good idea of the looks you can achieve with a brick patio. Note, too, that bricks set any one of several ways can serve as permanent borders for your patio.

Choosing and Buying Bricks

If you decide on bricks as the right patio surface for you, take a trip to one or more brick suppliers in your area. You'll be amazed by the selection. Not only will you find a huge number of standard-size bricks in many colors and textures, but you'll also encounter jumbo and irregular-shaped ones as well.

Once you make your selection, ask the supplier to estimate your needs (have the dimensions of the patio handy). For a 10x20-foot patio, you'll need approximately 920 standard-size bricks, including an allowance for breakage. And since bricks generally are sold in multiples of 500, you'll need two pallets of them.

The cost of bricks varies considerably, but for argument's sake, figure on each one costing from 15 to 25 cents. Delivery to the job site will cost you an additional amount.

Note: If you're a used-brick fan, be sure that the ones you purchase are hard; some will crumble when you crack them with a hammer. Also make certain that not too much mortar is sticking to them; mortar-encrusted bricks take a lot of work to clean.

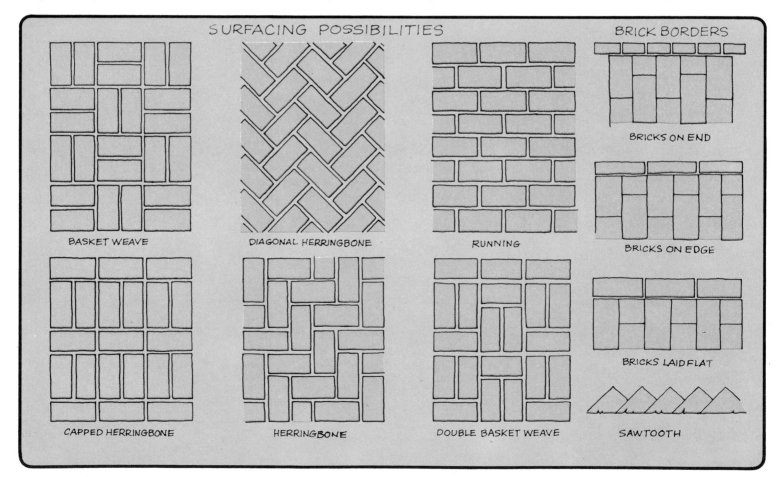

SURFACING POSSIBILITIES

BASKET WEAVE

DIAGONAL HERRINGBONE

RUNNING

BRICK BORDERS

BRICKS ON END

BRICKS ON EDGE

CAPPED HERRINGBONE

HERRINGBONE

DOUBLE BASKET WEAVE

BRICKS LAID FLAT

SAWTOOTH

Laying Bricks in Sand

Because the sand joints between bricks absorb water, eliminating drainage problems, you needn't do a lot of site preparation for a bricks-in-sand patio. However, the area should be fairly level, which may require some digging on your part. If you have large amounts of dirt to move, hire a grading contractor to solve the problem. As you shovel or grade, keep in mind that the bricks are laid over a two- to four-inch base of sand. Consider brick thickness, too. Both can affect the grade depth.

Setting up forms to define the patio's perimeter makes good sense even when setting bricks. Whether or not you want to use internal forms is a design consideration. See page 11 for help on setting up forms. If you plan to remove the forms after you complete the project, use economy-grade 1x6 or 1x8 boards. But if they'll be part of the design, be sure to use cedar, redwood, or pressure-treated wood, fastened together with galvanized nails.

If your project will be a weekend affair, order all the materials at once. But if you plan to take your time with the job, it's easy to work in sections.

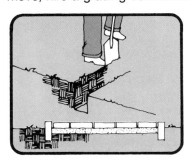

Stake out the area and level the surface. For patios with borders of bricks on end, also dig a trench along the perimeter.

Spray the ground with weed killer. Then cover the area with dark 4-mil polyethylene film. This will prevent most plant growth.

Now install the edging. Set bricks on end, edge, or flat. If you're using wood forms, stake them every 2½ feet.

Spread coarse sand to a depth of two to four inches. Level it as best you can with a shovel. Then sprinkle the area with water.

Work in sections about three feet square. Screed the sand using a 2x4 with the ends notched to fit over the edging.

Lay the bricks in the screeded area. Set them in position as carefully as possible, being careful not to disturb the sand.

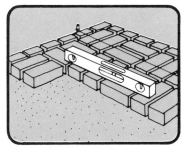

To help you lay the bricks level, stretch a mason's line. Also periodically check the units for level.

If you find a low brick, lift it out and sprinkle more sand underneath. If it's too high, remove the brick and some sand.

Cut the bricks with a brick chisel. Put the brick on a firm surface, score the break line with the chisel, and tap with a sledge.

After all bricks are set, spread shovelfuls of damp sand across the surface. Let it dry several hours, then sweep it into joints.

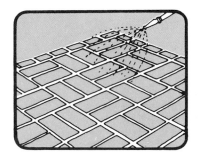

Wet the area thoroughly so the sand will settle into the joints. Use a fine spray to avoid forcing the sand from the joints.

You will have to repeat sanding and watering several times. After the cracks are full, let the surface dry and sweep it again.

WORKING WITH CONCRETE

If you haven't already played with what masons call "mud," prepare to encounter a new world of products, processes, and terminology. Start by getting the terminology straight.

First comes the mud itself. If, like most people, you've been calling it "cement," now's the time to change your vocabulary. *Cement* is a dry, powdery substance. Mix it with sand and water and you get *mortar,* the stuff used to bind brick, block, and stone walls together. (More about this on pages 36–43.) Adding gravel to a mortar mix makes *concrete*—a basic paving and structural material.

Any concrete-working project calls for a series of strenuous jobs. Usually you have to level off the area you'll be surfacing. Then you have to build temporary or permanent *forms* to hold the concrete while it sets. Next you have

to *place* the concrete—heavy work that also has to be done quickly, before the mix sets. Finally, you have to level *(screed)* the surface, *float* it to work out any irregularities, and *finish* it—again while the mud is still wet.

The following pages take you step by step through each of these stages. Because of the work involved, you may as well forget about tackling a huge project such as a driveway or king-size patio.

Start by checking community building codes. Many require a building permit —especially for a sidewalk or patio that will be attached to your home. If your project requires one, you'll be asked for information such as the size of the project, its location, approximate cost, and so on. There's often a small permit fee, too.

Also as part of the planning stage of your project, ask yourself the following questions.

Does a concrete truck have access to the job site? If not, have a couple of

wheelbarrows and some help on hand.

Must any electric or telephone lines be disconnected so a concrete truck can gain access to the site? If so, notify the utilities in advance.

Does the site require any special drainage? Usually, sloping or crowning the area can provide adequate water drainage. But problem drainage areas may require regular drain tile beneath the concrete.

Does the project require special grading? If so, check with utilities to make sure there are no buried utility cables or lines where you're digging.

Is special concrete reinforcement such as welded wire mesh or reinforcing rods needed? Driveways and walkways over which cars and trucks will be driven, and some patios attached to house foundations, require reinforcement. Generally, you should reinforce all concrete projects—even if traffic over them is light. Reinforcement helps protect the concrete from cracks, breaks, and other weather-induced problems.

Tools for Concrete Work

For most new concrete projects and many repair and maintenance jobs, you'll need the equipment illustrated here.

A *mason's hammer* will help drive form and alignment stakes; break stone, block, and brick; and chip away crumbling concrete. Lay out concrete-, brick-, and block-laying jobs with a *50-foot tape, mason's line,* and *line level.* For smoothing and finishing concrete, you'll need a *darby,* a *float* or a *bull float,* and a *finish trowel.* And to mix and distribute concrete, have a *hoe* and *shovel* on hand.

To help you distribute your weight over the fresh concrete so you don't sink into it, make a *knee board* from lumber or plywood. Use a *jointing tool* to divide and smooth concrete, such as the lines dividing a sidewalk into sections. An *edger* smooths and finishes the edges of concrete; use it while the forms are still in position. Quality concrete tools are affordable, so buy the best.

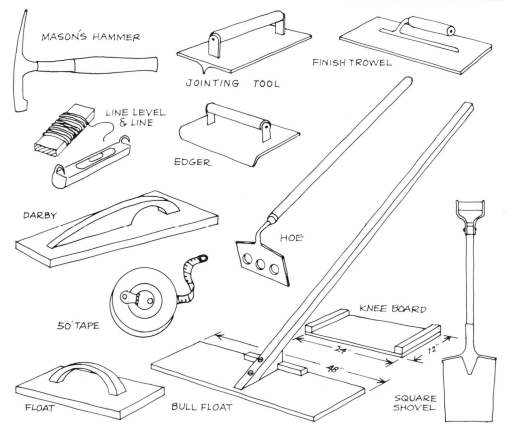

MASON'S HAMMER

JOINTING TOOL

FINISH TROWEL

LINE LEVEL & LINE

EDGER

DARBY

HOE

KNEE BOARD

24″

48″

12″

50′ TAPE

FLOAT

BULL FLOAT

SQUARE SHOVEL

BUILDING FORMS

Don't look at the task of building forms as a finish carpentry project. It's not. Here, strength is more important than good looks, so spend your extra effort on secure bracing. Concrete places a good amount of stress on forms, and having one or more of them give way while you're pouring is one of those disasters that happen all too often to do-it-yourself concrete workers.

The material used for forms varies, depending on the job. Economy-grade 2x4s work well for straight runs. For curves, use ¼-inch exterior plywood or tempered hardboard. A light coat of used motor oil applied to wood forms prevents them from sticking to the concrete and lets you recycle the lumber.

Most often, you'll want to disassemble and remove the forms after the concrete sets. To make this job easier and less time-consuming, secure the forms with double-headed nails. Allow the concrete to set a day or two before removing the forms (as it sets, it will change color—from a dark gray to its characteristic light gray color).

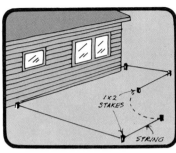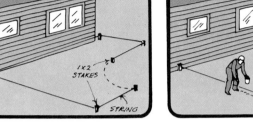

Locate the patio, adding two inches all around to accommodate forms. Stake off the outline, checking corners for square.

Transfer the outline to the ground by pouring sand over the mason's line. Carefully remove the stakes and the line guides.

Remove vegetation and excavate to allow for the sand bed and the slab. Excavate about one foot wider than the outline.

Level and tamp the excavated area, digging out rocks and roots and filling depressions. Wet the area to further compact the base.

Using a short length of forming to space the stakes, drive one every 24 to 30 inches. Scrap boards make good stakes.

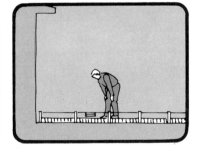

Establish grade by stretching a mason's line from the first to the last stake in each row. Pitch stakes slightly for drainage.

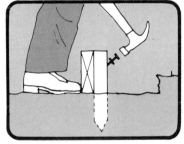

Secure the forms to the stakes with double-headed nails as shown. The stakes must be flush with or below the forms.

For curves, stake hardboard or plywood every 18 to 24 inches. You can outline the contour with a length of rope or garden hose.

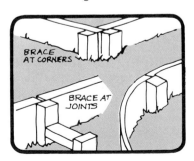

Brace the forms at each corner and at any weak spots. Stakes should be about 24 inches long and well set.

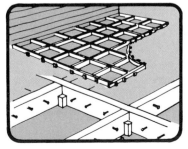

If you divide the patio into grids, stake the permanent inner forms as shown. Drive nails into forms to help hold the concrete.

Cedar, redwood, or pressure-treated boards make excellent permanent forms. Add reinforcing rods or mesh, if desired.

BUYING CONCRETE

Knowing what's available and the type suited to a particular job is the secret to concrete buymanship. Here's a brief rundown.

Ready-mix concrete. To order concrete, simply call one of the many concrete companies in your area, telling the personnel what you want the concrete to do, and the area of your project. It's as simple as that. But before you make that call, be sure you have prepared the site completely. Don't expect the person who delivers the concrete to sit around and watch you rebuild forms, place reinforcement mesh, or hunt for tools. Usually, excess time spent at a job results in an additional charge. Make sure, too, either that the truck has access to the site or that you have wheelbarrows on hand to transport the mix. Most ready-mix companies won't deliver less than one cubic yard of concrete, so keep this in mind when placing an order.

Premixed concrete. This product comes in bags. You simply add water and stir. Use this type for small jobs and repairs.

You-mix-it concrete. For large jobs, you should rent a concrete mixer; for small jobs and repairs, mix the material in a bucket or mortar box. The cost is fairly inexpensive, but you may have a cement, gravel, and sand storage problem.

Estimating How Much You Need

Figuring your concrete needs is one of those jobs that's much easier than most people imagine. Just apply a little mathematics.

If your project is rectangular or square, multiply the width by the length by the thickness of the job *in feet.* This gives you *cubic feet.* If you're purchasing ready-mix, then divide the result by 27, the number of cubic feet in a *cubic yard,* which is the unit in which concrete is sold.

To determine the area (in square feet) of a circle, multiply the square of the radius by 3.1416. Then, refer to the formula above to determine cubic measurements. And for triangular projects, multiply the length of the base by the perpendicular height, and divide the result by two.

For all irregular shapes, it's best to draw the project to scale on graph paper. Let each square represent one square foot. This way, you can count the full, half, and quarter squares and determine approximately how many square feet your project covers.

When dealing with ready-mix concrete companies, you probably will find that the salesman will want to know the area and the thickness of the concrete project—even if you furnish him with your estimate. Since mixing procedures vary somewhat, take the salesman's estimate—unless it's vastly out of agreement with your figures.

CONCRETE ESTIMATOR Expressed in both cubic feet and (cubic yards)				
Thick-ness	**Surface Area of Job In Square Feet**			
	20	50	100	200	500
2 in.	3.3 (.1)	8.3 (.3)	16.7 (.6)	33.3 (1.2)	83.3 (3.1)
4 in.	6.7 (.2)	16.7 (.6)	33.3 (1.2)	66.7 (2.5)	166.7 (6.2)
6 in.	10 (.4)	25 (.9)	50 (1.9)	100 (3.7)	250 (9.3)

Note: If the ground over which you'll pour the concrete is sloped and the finished work will be level, you must take into consideration the thickness of the concrete from the top of the slope to the bottom of it.

Choosing a Mix

The type of project you're undertaking determines the strength or "mix" of concrete you should blend or have mixed. Patios and sidewalks, for example, don't need the strength a footing or driveway does. And a thicker slab requires less cement proportionally than does a thinner one because of its greater mass.

For most home maintenance and improvement projects under normal conditions, the regular mix of three parts gravel mix to two parts sand to one part cement will give you the desired results. When mixed with water, this mixture contains enough cement powder to coat each particle of sand and gravel, and thereby create the bond that gives concrete its strength.

The amount of water added to the mixture is vitally important—use only enough to make the mixture workable. For more on this important aspect, see the opposite page. If you're mixing your own concrete, move the mixing container as close to your project as possible. Doing this allows you to keep the mixture thick and strong, yet workable.

If you're ordering ready-mix, specify a minimum bearing capacity of 3,500 psi (pounds per square inch) at 28 days' cure.

During inclement weather, it's advisable to add or ask for additives that speed curing times. These lessen the concrete's vulnerability to freezing, which weakens it.

MIXING CONCRETE

Mixing concrete is much like mixing cake batter: you have to follow the recipe (or adapt it slightly) to obtain the very best results. Just as you can ruin a cake by adding too much liquid, so too can you weaken concrete if you add too much water in proportion to the other materials. On the other hand, too little makes the concrete very difficult to pour and finish properly.

The amount of water needed depends largely on the condition of the sand you're using. You'll need to add less water to a mix made with wet sand than to one that uses drier sand.

Test the sand by balling some in your hand. If water runs out, the sand is very wet. If the ball compacts, like moist clay, the sand is perfect. And if the ball crumbles, the sand is too dry.

As you're mixing the concrete, add only very small amounts of water at a time. At the outset, the concrete may crumble, but as you add more water, it will begin to flow together like thick mud. When it becomes one color—a medium gray—and has a shiny, plastic-like sheen, it's ready to use.

Mix batches of concrete in a wheelbarrow, on a piece of plywood, or on any flat, water-proof surface you can hose off.

Measure the ingredients by the bucketful, leveling off the material with your shovel. Proper amounts are very important here.

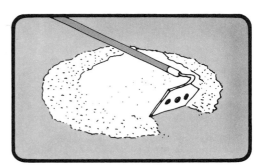

Use a concrete hoe or a shovel to thoroughly mix the right propor-tions of cement, sand, and gravel. Roll one into the other.

Make a well in the center of the pile and pour in water gradually, mixing the components to a thick, muddy consistency.

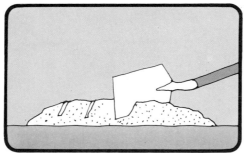

Test the batch first by smacking it with the back of a shovel. Then jab it lightly to make a series of grooves, as illustrated.

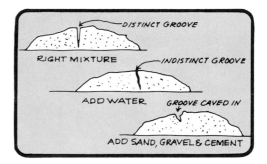

If the surface is smooth and the grooves maintain their separa-tion, the mix is right. If not, add water, or add more material.

Using a Power Mixer

If you need to mix lots of concrete, you should rent an electric- or gasoline-powered concrete mixer. These save many hours of hard labor.

To use a mixer, first add all of the gravel and some water, and switch on the mixer. Then add the sand, the cement, and finally, more water. Mix three minutes, gradually adding water until the mix achieves a uniform color. Stop the mixer often to test the batch, as shown above.

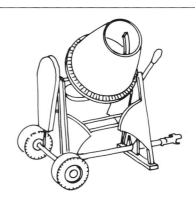

GETTING READY FOR A POUR

There's no better way to ensure a successful pour than to have everything ready when the concrete is. Conversely, few things can cause more aggravation than a hasty setup. So start a couple days early; do all of the preparation work listed and shown here.

• Make sure all forms are in the correct position, and drive all stakes flush with or below the top edge of the forms. If in doubt about the stability of the forms, add more stakes.

• Install expansion joints along the edges of foundations, other slabs, and other structural members. These expansion joints allow for daily movement of the concrete due to changes in temperature and humidity.

• Have utility companies remove any necessary wire or cable obstructions. Also make firm arrangements for having these reconnected.

• Assemble all necessary concrete tools—shovels, hoes, floats, trowels.

• Recruit several helpers, if the project calls for a large amount of concrete.

Fit expansion joints between the slab and any abutting structure, such as your foundation, and every 8 to 10 feet in slabs.

If you plan to reuse the forms, coat them with oil or shellac. If the forms will remain in place, protect the edges with masking tape.

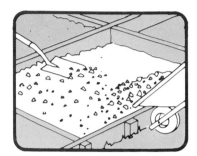

Make a bed for the concrete by spreading sand, cinders, or gravel. Generally, a couple inches of any of these will do.

Screed the base material to level the surface. Then tamp the base lightly so it's well compacted and completely level.

Use a heavy welded-wire mesh for reinforcement. Have a helper stand on one end, then unroll the mesh and cut it. Wear gloves.

If working with grids, cut the mesh to fit, then flatten it out by walking on it. Heavy bolt cutters make easy work of the cutting.

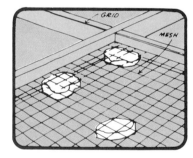

Lay the mesh into each grid and prop it up with rocks to about midway up the forms. Avoid walking on the mesh.

Wet down the area the day before pouring the concrete. Sprinkle it again just before pouring to slow the drying time.

GETTING READY FOR READY-MIX

A concrete truck weighs tons, and can ruin any walk or lawn over which it passes. If possible, have wheelbarrows ready to move the concrete or, if the project is within 18 to 20 feet of the street, have the truck park at curbside and chute the material to you. If necessary, you can spread out the weight of the truck by laying down planks.

Lay plywood or 1-inch-thick boards for wheelbarrow runs. Select a smooth route and have plenty of help on hand.

If the truck must roll over your lawn, make a road for it with 2-inch-thick lumber. Allow about 12 feet of overhead clearance.

PLACING CONCRETE

For all its strength, concrete is a delicate building material. You have to baby it before and after it's placed.

More than anything else, concrete needs sufficient time to cure. If you pour concrete over frozen ground, it will break up when the ground thaws. Pouring it over extremely dry ground is almost as bad—the water in the concrete mixture will be absorbed by the ground, "starving" the mix and setting it before you have a chance to finish it.

After the concrete has been poured, you'll notice a thin layer of water forming over the top of it. You may be tempted to remove the water with a broom or start troweling the concrete surface. Don't! The cement and aggregate in concrete are suspended by water. As gravity settles these "hard" materials, the water rises to the top of the mixture. If you trowel the surface now, it will "craze" and flake after the concrete has cured.

The proper sequence is to pour the concrete, strike or screed it, float it, and then trowel it. Do all of this quickly; if your project is a large one, have a couple of helpers available.

Begin pouring concrete in the least accessible area. Build a bridge, if you're wheelbarrowing the mixture.

Spread the concrete with a shovel or concrete hoe. Tamp the mixture so it's only a bit higher than the top edges of the forms.

Dump succeeding loads against the first one, not on top of it or separated from it. Pull up reinforcing mesh with rake tines.

Strike off the surface with a straight 2x4 after the concrete has been poured. See-saw the 2x4; fill low spots.

Floating further levels the surface and pushes aggregate beneath it. The float will produce a rough but level finish.

Float small areas with a darby, swinging the tool in an arc. Stop floating when water starts to bleed onto the surface of the slab.

When the surface appears "dry," test it by scraping it with a steel trowel. If wetness appears, don't finish the slab yet.

Sandwich a trowel blade between the form and concrete to separate them, then run an edging trowel along the form's edge.

Make control joints by laying a 2-inch board across the slab. Then run a jointing tool across the slab, using the board as a guide.

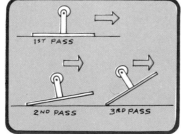
For a slick finish, trowel the surface three times. Move your arm in a wide arc and apply medium downward pressure to the tool.

A wooden trowel or float produces a rough, skidproof surface. It works like a steel trowel, but needs only one or two passes.

Cover the surface with sheets of polyethylene to hold moisture in the concrete. Or sprinkle it with water daily for one week.

CUSTOM-FINISHING CONCRETE

There's a little bit of the artist in us all, and there's no better time to vent some of that artistic energy than when surface-finishing your concrete project.

Duplicate one of the designs shown below or, if you're really feeling creative, dream up a design of your own. Decide on the surface you want in advance, though. You'll need all the time you can get to execute the design.

You might also consider coloring your concrete to achieve a special look.

Ready-mix companies will add coloring—usually red, brown, green, and black—for an additional charge. If you're mixing your own, purchase a coloring powder and mix it with the other ingredients as specified on the label.

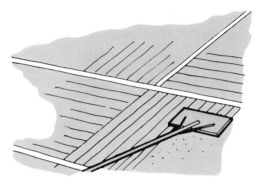

Swirl design. By working the trowel across the surface as shown above, you can produce this subtle, yet intriguing look. Using the edge of a steel trowel, lightly work the concrete, making sure that you don't dig the edges of the trowel into it. The swirls should be random; don't try to establish any particular pattern. Just "freewheel" the trowel, forming a series of interconnecting arcs. Texture the surface at control joints and edges, too, so they match the swirled texture, or leave the controls as is and let them define separate sections.

Checkerboard. This texture requires relatively little work. In fact, the less trowel work you do, the more interesting and skid-proof the final effect will be. Though especially attractive with a patio laid out in grids, checkerboarding will work on large expanses as well. Use a bull float, darby, or wood hand float as shown above. You also can buy floats with a sponge-like surface attached to them, which will create a more pronounced texture effect.

Brooming. For even more texture, treat the surface to a broom treatment after the concrete has been floated and has hardened somewhat. For a light texture, use a soft-bristled broom; for coarser effects, use a broom with heavy straw or steel bristles. You can create similar special effects with a bamboo lawn rake and a lawn rake with either close-set or wide-set tines. Use light pressure on the rake handle. It's smart, too, to test the design before total commitment. You can always re-trowel the surface and try something else.

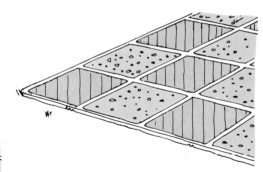

Exposed aggregate. Press the aggregate into the concrete with a wooden float, darby, or wide board until the pebbles are no longer visible. After the concrete begins to set, hose and scrub the surface with a stiff broom till you see the tops of the pebbles. Go easy, though; too much scrubbing will dislodge the pebbles. Let the concrete set for about three to four days, then wash the surface with a 1:5 solution of muriatic acid and water. Wear protective clothing, and rinse the area afterward.

Geometric. Actually, any series of lines meeting at random points would fall into this category of design. The sample shown here resembles the effect you'd get if you laid flagstones. A joint strike makes a perfect tool for embedding this design into the concrete. Use a light hand with it, though, as deep recesses in the surface readily collect dirt and other matter. Work the design after the surface has set long enough to support you on a knee board.

Combination effects. Don't rule out the possibility of combining two or more designs to come up with other unique surfaces. The one depicted above successfully combines exposed aggregates and a smooth troweled look. It's best to sketch out your ideas ahead of time so you're not taken by surprise when you start finishing the surface. Often, you can adapt or duplicate ideas found in magazines, outside public buildings, or on a neighbor's patio.

BUILDING A DECK

Most people would be scared stiff if faced with the prospect of building a deck. The reason: decks, especially well-constructed ones, look difficult to erect. A few are truly complex creations that require super-skilled hands to build, but most are well within reach of the average do-it-yourselfer. And that's the purpose of the next few pages—to make this entirely possible building project possible for you.

Using the right materials and providing adequate support are the two most important aspects of deck building. If the deck can't withstand the impact of weather, or if it's so shaky that no one feels comfortable on it, your hard work and money will go to waste.

Use only woods especially intended for outdoor use, and even then take special pains to protect them (see page 6 for information on applying protective coatings). And to ensure that the deck you raise is structurally sound, build it in compliance with the span tables at right and the building basics that follow.

BEAM AND JOIST SPAN TABLE		
Beam Size	**Maximum Distance Between Posts**	
4x6		6 ft.
4x8		8 ft.
4x10		10 ft.
4x12		12 ft.
Joist Size	**Span at Different Spacings**	
	16 in. 24 in. 32 in.	
2x6	8 ft. 6 ft. 5 ft.	
2x8	10 ft. 8 ft. 7 ft.	
2x10	13 ft. 10 ft. 8 ft.	

Getting Started

With a tape measure and six or eight 1x2 stakes, go out into the yard where you plan to build the deck. Determine the width and length of the structure, measuring these distances and staking them out. Also determine the height of the deck by measuring up the side of the house and marking where you want the top of the decking. These initial procedures visually tell you whether or not the deck site and the size are suitable for your needs. If you decide they aren't, shift the location, alter the size, or both.

Next, roughly design the deck on paper, using the actual staked-out measurements. Once you're happy with it, obtain any necessary building permits for the project.

Then, lay out the job. Mark the intended location of the ledger strip, which will support the joists at the house (not needed for freestanding decks). Build *batter boards* at the corners, using a mason's line to determine the height and squareness of the deck. To check the corners for square, measure three feet along the ledger strip mark and four feet down the mason's line. The distance between these two end points should be five feet, as the drawing shows. Also determine the location of all posts, using the chart above as a guide.

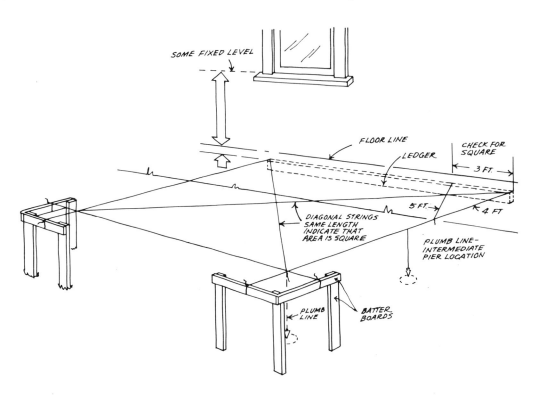

SOME FIXED LEVEL

FLOOR LINE

LEDGER

CHECK FOR SQUARE

3 FT.

5 FT.

4 FT.

DIAGONAL STRINGS SAME LENGTH INDICATE THAT AREA IS SQUARE

PLUMB LINE— INTERMEDIATE PIER LOCATION

PLUMB LINE

BATTER BOARDS

Setting Posts

Though you could find dozens of examples to the contrary, posts, unless pressure-treated wood, should be set directly in concrete or (preferably) on top of a concrete footing. Otherwise, they won't hold up for long.

If you set them in concrete, first pour a footing that is several inches larger than the post and that extends below the frost line (check with contractors in your area for proper depth). Unless the project is an unusually large one, you should be able to get by with using premixed bagged concrete rather than ordering ready-mix. While the concrete is still wet, set and level the post. Attach outrigger stakes to steady the post until the concrete sets.

To set posts on concrete, first pour the footing and position any one of the anchoring devices shown below in the still-workable concrete.

For most deck projects, 4 × 4 posts will provide adequate structural support. Just be sure you get them plumb (check each twice, taking readings on sides at right angles to each other) and in perfect alignment with each other. For more information about erecting posts, turn to pages 26–28.

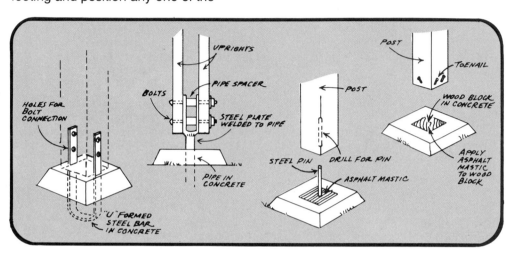

Set posts in concrete as shown above. Tapering the concrete at ground level helps shed water, which otherwise collects here.

Any one of the above anchoring devices will serve as a stable post anchor. Also available are adjustable post bases that fit over machine or carriage bolts that have been set in the concrete footing or slab. These allow for making minor lateral adjustments.

Attaching the Beams

As you can see from the sketch at right, you have several perfectly sound alternatives for attaching beams. If you plan to run the posts up through the decking to serve as supports for the deck's railing, fashion the beams of two lengths of 2x material and sandwich the posts between them.

If your deck is an on-grade type, in which case you won't need a railing, you'll want to cut the posts to the correct height and fasten the beams atop them.

For maximum strength, it's best to use bolts or large wood screws to anchor the beams. The movement so characteristic of decks works nails loose too easily.

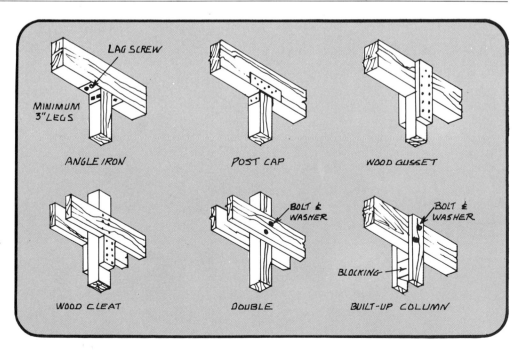

Attaching Ledgers and Joists

Unless your deck is freestanding and depends on posts as its primary source of support, you must somehow fasten a ledger strip—usually a 2x8 or 2x10—to your house. The first three sketches below show your fastening options.

Regardless of which you choose, bear in mind that all vertical measurements must allow for the thickness of the decking you'll be using.

Before drilling the holes for the fasteners, decide whether you want the joists to rest atop the ledger or flush with it as would be the case if you're using joist hangers. For joist hangers, make certain that when positioned, the bottom of the ledger is level with the top of the beams toward the outer edges of the

deck. Double-check the ledger's intended position by running a string with a line level from the top of the beam to the house. With your measurements thus confirmed, attach the ledger, making sure that it's level.

The joists come next. The size you need for your project depends on the spans involved, but 2x6s, 2x8s, and 2x10s are most common. If you're using joist hangers, nail them along the ledger, usually at 16-inch intervals. Then position the joists on the beams and in the hangers and secure them. If you're setting the joists on the beams and ledger, toenail them into position with galvanized nails.

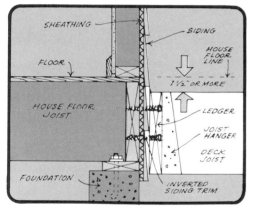

To attach a ledger strip to the house framing, use lag screws. If the house has lap siding, invert a piece for a shim.

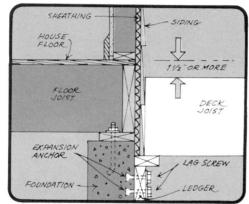

To fasten ledgers to a foundation, use lag screws and expansion anchors. The joists rest on top of the ledger strip unit.

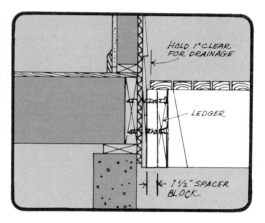

You'll need to install flashing to protect the ledger. Or, space the ledger 1½ inches from the house so water can run through.

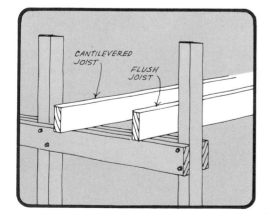

Joists can be cantilevered over the beam, or flushed. You might prefer the cantilevered effect if you don't skirt the deck.

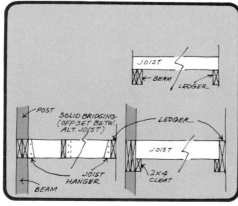

Rest joists on top of the ledger and beam, then toenail them. Or make them flush by butt-joining, or cleating and toenailing.

Constructing Stairs

Laying out a stairway is one of the most challenging of all carpentry jobs. Not only do you have to accurately compute angles, you must also maintain equal riser and tread spacing from top to bottom.

Building an open-riser/open-stringer stairway such as the one illustrated here provides an excellent, relatively easy introduction to this advanced task.

Start by thinking of stairs as a means of dividing a difference of elevation into a series of equal steps. Then, measure this distance (the *total rise*) as well as the distance from your deck to where you want the stairs to end (the *total run*).

Generally, each step has a rise of about seven inches and a run of 10 or 11 inches. Divide these figures into the total rise and run to find out if they give you an even number of steps. Chances are, they won't. If so, adjust the individual rise and run measurements until you do come out even. Don't forget to include the thickness of the tread material you'll be using in your rise computations.

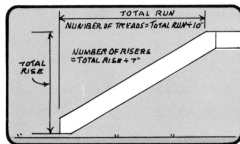

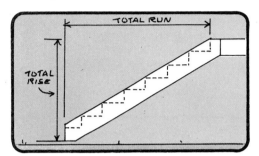

To determine total rise and run, measure height from the top of the deck to the ground, and from the deck to where stairs will end.

Take these figures and divide them by the standard rise and run figures given above to determine the number of steps required.

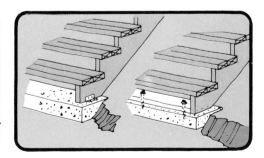

Next, mark off the riser height on one leg of a framing square and the depth of the tread on the other leg of the square.

Lay the square against a 2x10 or 2x12, then scribe the marked points onto the lumber as illustrated here.

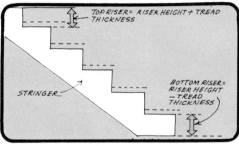

Tread thickness affects the height of the first and last steps. Subtract this thickness from the bottom; add it to the top.

Use the first cut stringer as a template for the second and/or third stringer. Be sure that you allow for the saw kerf here.

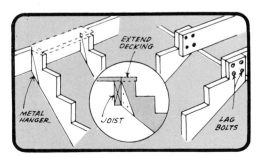

Fasten the stringers to the sides of a joist or header using a metal hanger. Or you can bolt the steps to the ends of joists.

Next, nail on the treads, using large galvanized finishing nails. Cut tread material flush with the stringer or let it overlap.

Set the bottom of the steps on a concrete footing and fasten it with expansion anchors and lag screws or angle irons.

Laying Decking

It's when you nail the decking material to the joists that you'll begin to see what an attractive outdoor living area you've been erecting. And since the decking is one of the most visible of your deck's elements, it's very important that you lay it correctly.

Most people run the decking in one direction (across the joists), as it not only yields an attractive look, but also is the easiest design to lay. But with a little more work, you also can create a number of special-effect surfaces. You might, for example, want to fashion a parquet block design or run the decking diago-nally. Just keep in mind that you'll need adequate joist support beneath.

As for the materials to use, choose 2x2s, 2x4s, or 2x6s. Most people go with 2x4s. Use galvanized nails to secure the decking to the joists.

When laying that first piece (start at the house and work outward), make certain that it's square to the house. This first piece serves as the all-important guide for the rest of the decking. Use ¼-inch spacers to separate all subsequent pieces, and after laying every three or four strips, double-check for square by running a line from the house to both ends of the same piece of decking. Butt the ends of the decking pieces together for a snug fit.

Always check the end grain of each board before you nail it. You'll notice that the tree rings hump toward one side of the board—called the *bark side.* Nail all decking bark-side-up to minimize cupping.

If the lumber you're using is slightly warped, nail one end of it to a joist, then "pull" the loose end into position and nail it, working from joist to joist.

Should you notice the decking splitting as you're nailing it, try blunting the nail points slightly with a hammer. Or drill pilot holes for the nails, especially at the ends of the lumber where splitting usually occurs.

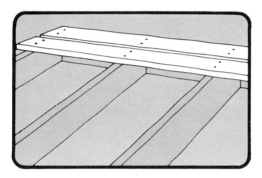

Drive two nails into the decking at every joist. And don't worry about cutting the decking to the exact length yet.

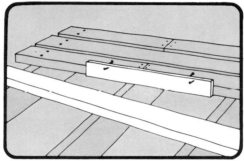

Maintain proper spacing between decking with a ¼-inch spacer strip. Stagger the end joints as you go across the deck.

After all the boards are nailed, snap a chalk line along the edges and trim them with a saw. Nail on a board as a guide strip.

Building Railings

Deck railings can be almost any design you want—as long as the design relates in scale to the deck and the structure adjoining it. But keep in mind that a railing's primary purpose is to provide safe passage from the deck to the ground. So build it strong, and if children will frequent the deck, position the rails close together.

The sketches below show three typical railing options. Duplicate one of them or, if you'd rather, dream up a one-of-a-kind treatment.

Secure all railing posts to the decking superstructure with lag screws or carriage bolts. Nails don't provide the needed holding power. And tie the railing in with the structure's posts, beams, or joists; don't rely on the decking strips to properly hold it in place.

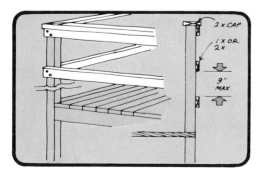

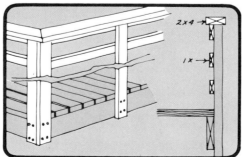

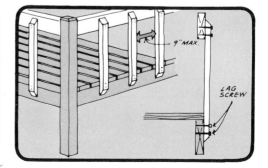

FENCES AND GARDEN WALLS

Examine the anatomy drawing below and you'll see a skeleton common to almost any non-masonry fence. *Posts*—at ends, corners, gates and "along the line"—support *rails* top, bottom, and sometimes in the center.

Individuality comes when you add *screening* (pickets are shown here, but there are dozens of other possibilities, too). To learn about the many shapes a fence can take and how to build one, see pages 24–30.

Build a masonry fence and you've got what's known as a *screen wall;* position it to hold back a slope, and it's a *retaining wall.* More about both beginning on page 31.

ANATOMY OF A FENCE

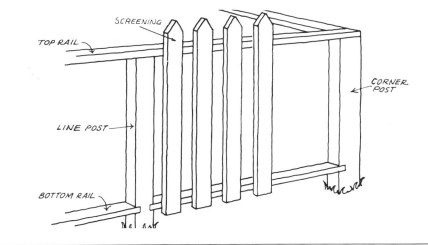

SCREENING

TOP RAIL

CORNER POST

LINE POST

BOTTOM RAIL

SOLVING FENCE PROBLEMS

REPAIRING DAMAGED RAILS

Rot—a fence's worst enemy—typically attacks bottom-rail joints first. Catch decay early and you can saturate the damaged spot with a preservative (see page 27), then mend it as shown below. If the rail has broken away, you'll have to replace it with treated wood.

To minimize rot around your fences, cut back surrounding vegetation; plants often serve as a poultice that holds moisture in the wood.

ROTTED SECTION

Shore up rotted rails with a short length of 2x4. Butt it tightly against the rail and fasten to post with galvanized nails.

Or secure rails to posts with galvanized steel T-braces. Drill pilot holes for screws, and paint the brace to match the fence.

Apply a liberal amount of butyl caulk at the rail/post joint. It will remain flexible to deter rot for several years.

SHORING UP (OR REPLACING) A WOBBLY POST

Usually, fence posts wobble either because they weren't properly set or treated to begin with, or because moisture, freezing, and thawing have loosened their buried ends.

If the posts are still in fairly good condition, you often can steady a wobble with stakes or splints, as shown in the sketches below.

If the posts have rotted away at ground level, you'll have to replace them—a big job since the rails and screening usually have to be dismantled and reassembled.

To remove posts, your best bet is to rent a post puller. Or, if you're willing to work harder, try inching them out of the ground with a long wrecking bar, using a piece of 4x4 for more leverage. Digging away the earth around the posts with a spade will make the prying and pulling job easier.

Install replacements as you would new posts (see pages 26–28). If possible, use pressure-treated lumber, clear all-heart redwood, or cedar. Failing this, treat the bottoms of the posts with a preservative before setting them into the ground. Also double-check your measurements. Enlarging the holes may have put spacings slightly off.

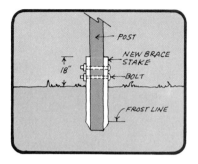

An easy way to shore up posts is with 2x4 stakes. Bevel driving ends; apply a preservative. Drive stakes; bolt together.

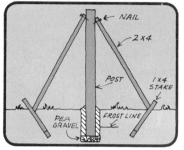

Concrete makes a more permanent repair. Enlarge postholes; pour concrete; tamp it. Braces keep posts plumb while you work.

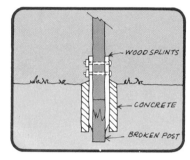

Mend posts broken below the ground with aluminum or wood splints. Enlarge hole; position and bolt splints; pour concrete.

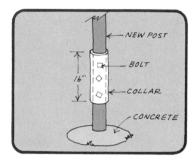

To repair rusted-out pipe posts, cut near ground level. Replace with new pipe, using a pipe collar and bolts to secure joint.

LIFTING A SAGGING GATE

Kids swinging on a garden gate can make it sag, but so can wobbly gate or line posts, loose hinges, or an out-of-square gate frame.

Sometimes excessive moisture can make a wooden gate swell, forcing it out of alignment. The tendency then is to jam the gate to open or close it, which loosens the hinges and causes the gate to sag when the moisture finally leaves the wood.

Metal gates sag because the posts are wobbly, or the pins that hold the gate to the post are bent.

Troubleshoot sagging gate problems by first checking gate posts to make sure they're firmly anchored in the ground and are plumb. If they're not, shore them up with one of the methods illustrated above.

If the posts are straight but the gate is binding, examine the hinges. Chances are, they're loose, worn, bent, or aren't heavy enough to support the weight of the gate. If so, replace them; don't attempt a repair.

If the gate is hung on a masonry wall or post, remove hinges and shim them as shown. If the latch side binds, plane it.

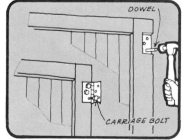

If hinges are loose, remove screws and fill holes with dowel plugs. Replace hinges using longer screws or carriage bolts.

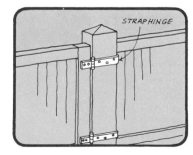

Replace worn hinges with larger ones. To make a strap hinge even stronger, bend its tip around a corner of the post.

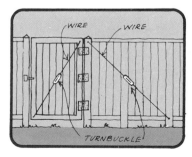

True-up out-of-square gate frames with heavy-duty turnbuckles and wire. Attach wire to screw eyes in the gate or fence framework.

BUILDING NEW FENCES

Thinking about putting up a new fence? If so, you have a satisfying project in store. But don't underestimate the amount of time and effort involved in building it—it's hard work!

Luckily, though, erecting a fence isn't complex. If you are reasonably handy and if you heed the advice given on the next few pages, you won't have much difficulty. No special skills are involved.

PLANNING A FENCE

As with so many other home improvement projects, the building of your fence is only one part of the project.

The up-front time involved in planning is equally important.

One of the first things you need to do is to check the building codes in your community. Many ordinances specify the maximum height a fence may be, distances you can build from property lines and the street, even materials you can and can't use.

Learn, too, whether you'll be required to have a building permit. (If the fence will protect a swimming pool, for example, you almost certainly will.) To apply for a permit, you'll have to submit a plan for authorities' approval. Pick up the forms and relevant regulations from your local building department.

If your new fence will abut neighbors' properties or affect their views, discuss your plans with them as well. Double-check property lines (hire a surveyor if you're uncertain where they are), and clarify who will maintain the fence.

As you develop a design, consider what you want your fence to do. Must it mask trash cans or a work area? Provide

privacy or security? Define a garden or patio? Screen the sun or buffer wind? A well-planned fence often can do several of these jobs at once.

Try, too, to visualize your design in context with present or future landscaping and outdoor living areas. Will you need a gate? As an alternative, consider building a series of freestanding fence panels staggered in such a way that they provide privacy yet let people walk through easily.

Choose materials and styling that will complement your home's appearance. If a new fence will be visible from the street, it also should harmonize with your neighborhood's character.

Proper scale is important, too. A too-tall fence, for instance, will visually overwhelm a low ranch house. You'll have a scale problem with a squatty fence beside a tall house.

BUFFERING WIND

Fences—like airplanes, bridges, and automobiles—are subject to some surprising principles of aerodynamics. It might seem, for instance, that a solid fence would make an excellent windbreak. But as you can see from the sketches below, solid construction could

actually aggravate a wind problem. What's more, a severe storm might flatten the entire fence.

If the winds in your area blow strong and often, slow them down with open-work screening such as slats, latticework, or bamboo. Louvers not only reduce the air's velocity considerably, they redirect it as well. Trees and shrubbery help control wind, too.

Before you orient a windbreak, check with the local weather bureau for the direction and severities of prevailing currents. If you happen to live in a rural area, ask your local extension service personnel for advice.

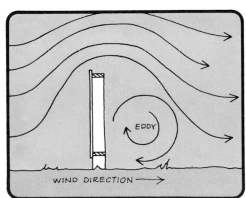

Wind that strikes a solid fence tends to "hop" over it, creating a vacuum on the lee side that pulls the air down again.

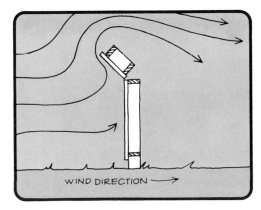

By adding a 45-degree baffle or cap at the top of the fence, you can greatly increase the wind-protected area on the other side.

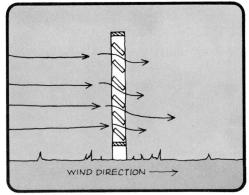

An open-work fence won't totally block the wind, but most types slow its velocity to a more comfortable level.

COPING WITH A SLOPE

Don't let a sloping or an up-and-down site discourage you from building a fence. In fact, building on uneven terrain often makes a fence more interesting visually than if it were straight-out level.

The drawings below show two ways to go, depending largely upon the slope's severity. For the first one, you'll have to "rack" the rails as you install them. Here's how that's done.

First sink the end posts, stretch a line between them, and lay out the rails to locate positions for the line posts, as illustrated on pages 26 and 28. Now dig a hole for the first line post and sink it; make this one several inches taller than the fence will be.

Next, fasten rails to the end post and pull them up or push them down until they're parallel to the ground. Fasten them to the line post. Repeat this procedure down the line.

After you've put up all the rails, go back and trim off the post tops to the proper height. Cut them at an angle so that rain and snow will not have a chance to collect there.

Let the fence follow the land's contour on a gentle slope. Open fence styles are better suited to this than solid ones.

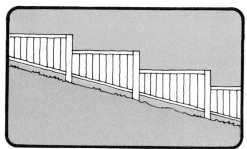

For steeper grades or fencing with solid screening, step the fence. Construct one section at a time—one post to the next.

CHOOSING A STYLE

Let function and personal preference guide you in your selection of a fence style. Chances are, you have some general style in mind now, but it might be worthwhile to look around to see how other people have handled their fencing needs. And don't overlook the ideas that abound in books and magazines, one of which you might like to duplicate or modify somewhat.

You may also find that lumberyard or home center personnel will be able to help you choose a style. They usually have a good idea of what styles of fences will work well in various situations.

In addition, study the typical styles that are shown below. Many of them are sold in prefab form, which saves a lot of cutting and fitting.

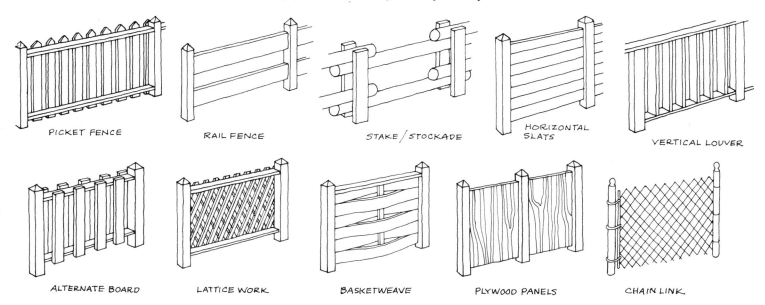

PICKET FENCE   RAIL FENCE   STAKE / STOCKADE   HORIZONTAL SLATS   VERTICAL LOUVER

ALTERNATE BOARD   LATTICE WORK   BASKETWEAVE   PLYWOOD PANELS   CHAIN LINK

LAYING OUT A FENCE

Take plenty of time for this phase of your fence-building project. The reason: a measurement that's just an inch off at the outset can compound itself into feet down the line.

Start by establishing positions for end and corner posts, then stretch lines between them. Now step back and look at your layout from several angles. If it looks good, sink end posts, then locate positions for the line posts.

Make measurements with a 50-foot tape. For stakes, use 1x2s or 2x2s that have been pointed with a hatchet.

Locate the terminal posts (corners and ends). Mark them with stakes. Then locate gate posts, and stake their positions.

Square the corners, using the 3-4-5 method. The square of the hypotenuse must equal the sum of the squares of the sides.

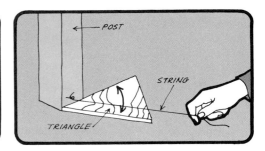

If a corner won't be 90 degrees, compute angle on graph paper and cut it from plywood scrap. Stretch lines on legs of angle.

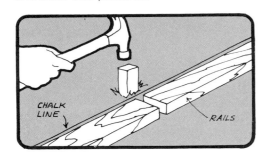

Locate the line posts by laying rails on the ground along the chalk line. Then drive the stakes where the rail ends butt.

For a stepped fence, plumb lower post in two directions. Use a tape measure to pinpoint stakes for line posts.

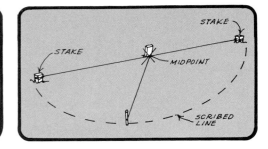

For a curved fence, stake ends. Stretch a line between them and find midpoint. Then trace circle with a line-and-stick compass.

DIGGING POSTHOLES

Generally speaking, if you set fence posts from 24 to 30 inches into the ground, they'll provide all the strength the fence will need. Of course, it's best to go below the frost line, but this usually isn't practical.

Sink terminal and gate posts slightly deeper than line posts. And to give yourself some leeway for getting everything plumb, make holes considerably larger than the posts.

Always set terminal and gate posts first. Then dig a hole for the first line post, set it, and move on to the next. Space six to eight feet apart.

If you have to dig just a few holes in rock-free earth, rent an auger (right) or clamshell-type digger for the job.

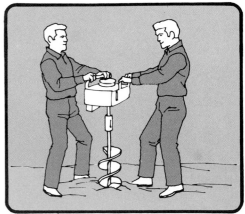

If you have a lot of holes to dig, rent a power-driven auger. These generate lots of torque, so you'll need a helper.

WARDING OFF DECAY

Rot will eventually destroy any wood fence, but you can retard decay for years by using redwood or cedar for any part that will be belowground. Or buy pressure-treated lumber that has been saturated with preservatives. A third, less desirable possibility is treating untreated lumber yourself (see below). Aboveground elements of the fence must be treated, too—but here applying a couple coats of paint or stain generally will get you by.

Setting posts in concrete slows down the decay process, but treat them anyway. Coat metal fences with rust-preventing primer and paint.

If you choose to use a material such as canvas for screening, figure on replacing it every few years.

COMPARING PRESERVATIVES		
Preservative	**Use/Application**	**Cost**
Creosote	For buried wood. Has a strong, medicinal smell and can't be painted over. Apply by dipping; provide plenty of ventilation.	Inexpensive
Pentachlorophenol	For buried wood. Can be painted. Harmful to plants until thoroughly dry. Paint two coats or dip.	Inexpensive
Copper naphthenate	Good for buried and aboveground lumber. Odorless, nontoxic. Gives wood a greenish look. Paint two coats or dip.	Moderate
Asphalt roofing compound	For buried wood. Paint three coats, allowing plenty of drying time between them.	Inexpensive
Exterior paints and stains	OK above ground, but almost useless below. Stains can be dipped.	Moderate

APPLYING PRESERVATIVES

With a nail or punch, poke a series of holes around the post at grade level. This allows more preservative to soak into wood.

If dipping many components, pour preservative into a drum. Soak enough of the post to extend 6 inches above grade.

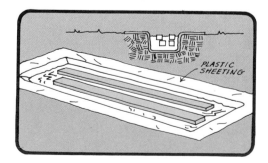

Or soak material in a shallow trench lined with a protective layer of polyethylene. Soak three days to ensure absorption.

Be sure to give special attention to post tops and areas where you've made cuts. Wear protective clothing while applying.

After you've assembled all of the posts and rails, give them another coat. Also treat any newly exposed wood.

SETTING FENCE POSTS

For strength and long life, set terminal posts (at ends, corners, and gates) in concrete. You can anchor line posts in soil unless the fence will be extremely tall, heavy, or subjected to strong winds (see page 26 for posthole-digging help).

Since the posts are set one at a time, consider buying premixed concrete for the job. The premixed material already has the proper amount of sand and gravel added to the cement; all you need to do is add water and mix.

The other choice is to buy the cement in bags, order sand and gravel, and mix the materials yourself (see pages 12 and 13). Be sure to order extra gravel for the bottom of the postholes. Although premixed concrete is more expensive than cement, sand, and gravel, the convenience usually is well worth the extra money spent.

Tools required for the job include a wheelbarrow or mixing box for concrete, spade, chalk line, line level, shovel, and steel trowel.

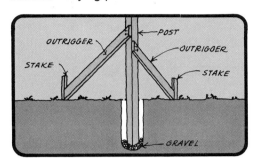

Shovel 2 to 3 inches of gravel in hole for first post. Set post in place; plumb it in two directions, bracing with outriggers.

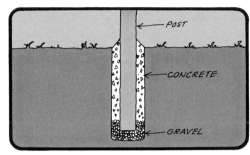

Add gravel around post. With a shovel, pour concrete, tamping each shovelful with a pipe to remove air bubbles in the mix.

Set next terminal post. Plumb and brace it. Stretch line between posts to ensure equal heights. Then add concrete.

To square gate openings, measure between the posts at top and bottom. Equal measurements mean a square opening.

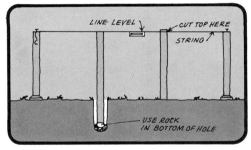

If you've accidentally dug a posthole too deep, use a rock as a filler. Dig shallow holes deeper or saw off post top later.

To set posts in soil, first lay down a gravel base, then have a helper shovel dirt into the hole while you tamp. Mound earth.

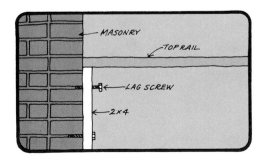

To attach a fence to a masonry wall, use lead expansion anchors and lag screws. A star drill punches holes for the anchors.

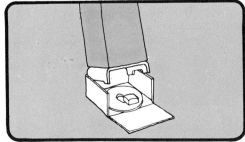

To fasten posts to a concrete slab, use metal post anchors, held in place with expansion anchors and lag screws.

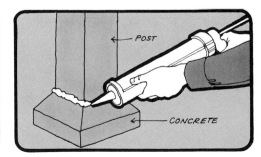

For a watertight seal around posts set in concrete, wait until a dry spell and apply butyl caulk where concrete meets post.

APPLYING FINISHES

Remember Tom Sawyer and his white-washing project? He quickly discovered that it takes a lot of time to work a brush into all of a fence's nooks and crannies . . . and since you have to coat both sides and most of the edges of all components, even a short fence can soak up a surprisingly large quantity of paint or stain.

Unless you're like Tom and have some gullible friends, your best bet is to finish a fence *before* you assemble it. After the posts are set, cut the rails and screening. Then lay them out on sawhorses or some other type of support system and apply the finish of your choice with a roller or a paintbrush.

Use any good exterior paint or stain. Both wood and metal should be primed first; this properly seals the surface so that the top coating will hold up longer under exposure to severe weather.

Spraying goes even faster, but the overspray wastes a lot of finish. Also, if you're not careful, you may kill nearby vegetation or get windblown paint on surrounding houses and cars.

Once a prefinished fence is assembled, you'll have to go back and touch up spots that have been marred by hammer tracks, saw cuts, and other knocks and dings. Just to be on the safe side, apply a third coat to the tops of the posts and to the joints between the rails and the posts.

PUTTING UP RAILS

Fastening rails to posts calls for only very simple joinery techniques. Once the posts are plumb and aligned, you simply cut each rail squarely, fasten it to one post, then level and attach it to the next.

The illustrations below show seven different ways to secure rails. Which one you choose depends upon your tools and skills. It's tough, for instance, to cut dadoes, notches, and mortise-and-tenons without power equipment. On the other hand, butt joints supported by blocks or metal angles call for only regular hand tools and little nailing know-how. Toenailed joints are easy, too, once you've mastered the knack of making them.

For fasteners, always use galvanized nails, screws, or bolts. Other types will stain the finish.

Space bottom rails at least six inches above the ground—far enough away so that vegetation doesn't transfer moisture to wood or metal parts. You may want to put them a little higher to make mowing easier. And taller fences may need a third rail spaced equally between top and bottom members.

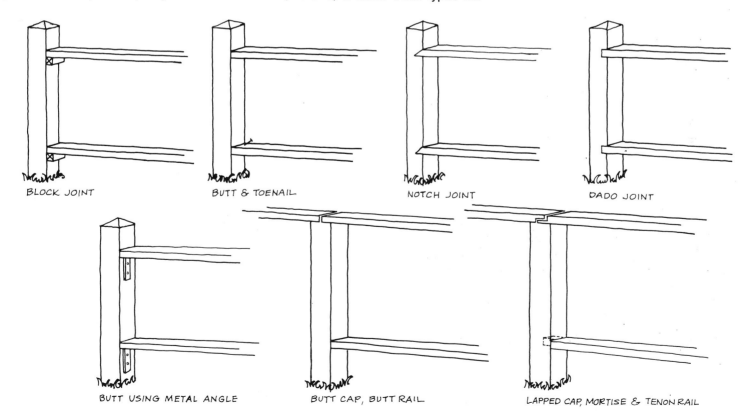

BLOCK JOINT

BUTT & TOENAIL

NOTCH JOINT

DADO JOINT

BUTT USING METAL ANGLE

BUTT CAP, BUTT RAIL

LAPPED CAP, MORTISE & TENON RAIL

29

PUTTING UP SCREENING

Now comes the fun part of building a fence—fleshing it out with screening material. As with any carpentry project, you must keep the parts square and level, so take your time putting them all together.

You can buy precut fence screening such as pickets, wooden panels, metal mesh panels, and gates. Other types of screening must be custom made: you have to cut, fit, and fasten on the pieces—an easy but repetitious job. For a custom fence, adapt the basic screening techniques shown below.

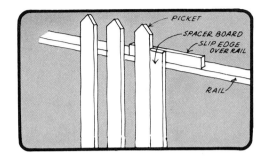

To space pickets, slats, and boards, rip a strip to the right width and nail a cleat to one end. Hang cleat on top rail.

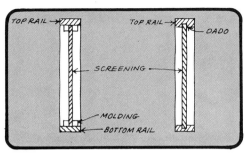

Nail screening to the sides of posts and rails. Sandwich it between molding strips, or fit it into dadoes in the rails.

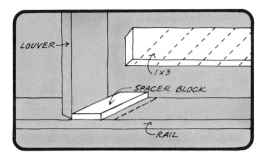

For a louvered fence, cut dozens of spacer blocks from 1x3 boards. Cut at 45-degree angles so each louver fits perfectly.

BUILDING A GATE

A gate that is strong and true will give you years of trouble-free service; a poorly constructed one will cause all kinds of grief. Hang the gate *before* attaching screening so you can correct an out-of-square opening.

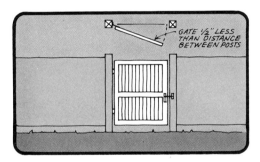

Square opening (see page 28). Make the frame ½ inch narrower than the opening. For very heavy gates, allow ¾ inch.

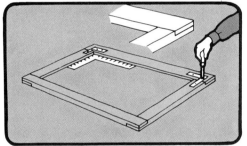

Use butt or lapped joints at corners of frame. Metal angle plates add strength at corners. Check square when assembling.

Brace the frame with a diagonal piece of wood that runs from the hinge side (top) to the latch side (bottom). Add screening.

Screw or bolt the hinges to the gate and prop gate in the opening. Fasten hinges to the post and add the latch hardware.

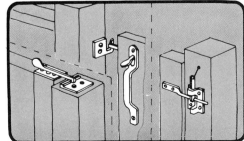

You can mount latches on the top or side of the gate. Three types are shown here. The thumb latch (center) requires boring to install.

With the gate closed, mark its inside edge on the latch post, then nail up a strip of wood to serve as a stop for the gate.

SOLVING WALL PROBLEMS

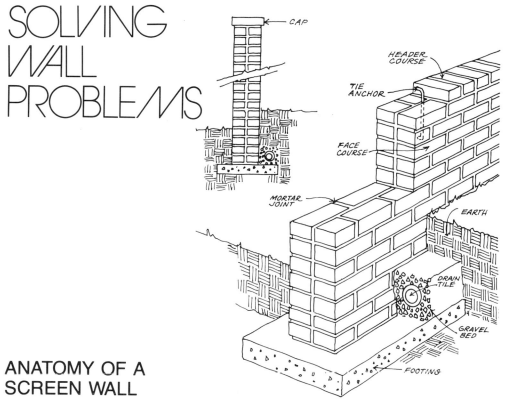

Garden walls fall into two broad categories: *screen walls,* which are really little more than masonry fences, and *retaining walls,* which hold back a slope and prevent erosion.

Both usually stand on concrete *footings,* and consist of successive *courses* of bricks, blocks, stones, or other material. Usually, *mortar*—a mixture of cement, sand, and water—binds the courses together. An exception is dry wall construction, shown on page 35. Brick walls, such as the one shown in the sketch at left, ordinarily have two or more *tiers,* interlocked periodically with metal *wall ties.*

Many walls are topped with a concrete or stone *cap.* Below, there may be a drainage system to carry off water.

Freezing and thawing water can heave footings, crumble mortar joints, and topple caps. So, check masonry walls twice a year. Pay particular attention to the situation at ground level.

Maintain and repair garden walls as you would any exterior masonry (see pages 32 and 33).

ANATOMY OF A SCREEN WALL

ANATOMY OF A RETAINING WALL

Retaining walls include the same basic elements as screen walls, plus a few additional features. *Reinforcing rods,* in addition to being used to strengthen the wall itself, also help tie the wall to the earth it retains. And *weep holes* provide a place for excess water to escape, keeping pressure off the wall.

Water is a retaining wall's mortal enemy, so do whatever's necessary to make sure the wall can shed it. Inspect your walls twice yearly. Trouble points include blocked drainage tiles and weep holes, erosion along the hill or slope, and erosion directly in back of the retaining wall where it meets the earth. Plantings and additional buried drainage tile will help stop erosion.

Keep mortar joints in masonry walls in repair by tuck-pointing them; patch damaged wall caps; and if the wall is wood, replace any rotting wood members with specially treated lumber.

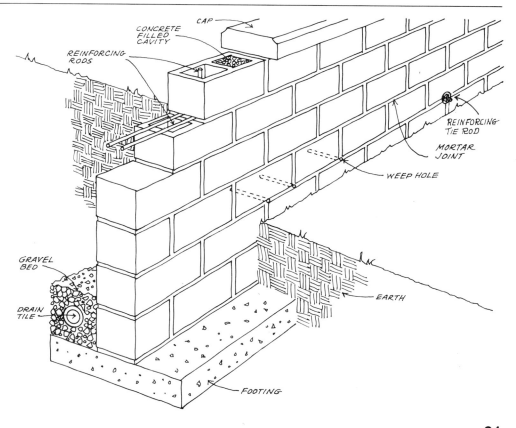

31

REPAIRING BRICKWORK

Though strong and durable, brick walls require occasional attention to keep them in good repair. Their most common malady: crumbling mortar. You can repair deteriorated joints by tucking mortar into them with the point of a trowel—a process masons call *pointing* or *tuck-pointing*.

To do the job, you'll need a couple of specialized tools. One is a *pointing trowel*, which is slightly smaller than an ordinary masonry trowel. The other is a

hawk, which you can buy or improvise by screwing a short length of dowel or broom handle to a square of plywood.

Pack the joints with mortar mixed with a liquid latex binder. You also can use conventional mortar mix (see page 36) or vinyl patching cement, which is easier to apply but doesn't look like mortar.

After you have filled and smoothed the joints, *strike* or shape them to match existing joints. (For typical mortar treatments, see page 41.)

You also can point long vertical cracks whether they involve the joints or the bricks themselves. A better solution is

to *grout* them as shown opposite, above. Don't overlook a broken brick, either (opposite, below); the freezing and thawing of any water it admits could cause more extensive damage.

With any masonry repair, it's important to keep the mortar damp for several days—rapid drying weakens the bond. Mist the repair with a hose, or cover with wet burlap.

Pointing Bricks

Clean out all loose mortar to a depth of about ¾ inch, making sure that what's left is tight. Take care not to chip the brick.

Brush the joints with a wire or scrub brush, then wet them down so the bricks won't draw water from the mortar.

Mix mortar to a consistency that will slide slowly off your trowel. Pick up by slicing off a hunk and slipping trowel under.

Pack mortar into the joint with the trowel's tip, then slice off the excess. A hawk lets you bring mortar right to the work.

After pointing 8 to 10 bricks, go back and scrub the joints with a soft, wet brush. This further compacts the mortar.

Strike the joints with the appropriate tool (see page 41). Dampen periodically for the next two or three days.

Grouting Long Cracks

Before filling a vertical crack like the one at right, first determine if the wall is settling. If you're satisfied that it's not, follow this procedure: loosen any clinging material with a knife or small screwdriver, then remove all debris from the crack with a vacuum.

With this done, force grout into the crack with a pointing trowel. Use a vinyl-based grout, as this type has the elasticity necessary to ride out expansion and contraction. Finish by striking grout.

Replacing a Damaged Brick

If yours is an older home, the most difficult part of this job will be finding a brick that harmonizes with its neighbors. Match colors by chipping out a piece and taking it to a dealer who specializes in used brick. Note the dimensions of your bricks, too; sizes vary.

For the work, you'll need mortar, a broad bricklayer's chisel, a heavy hammer or mallet, a trowel, and a tool for striking joints (see page 41). When working with the hammer and chisel, protect your eyes with goggles and your chisel hand with a leather work glove—misses hurt.

The illustrations at right show how to replace a full brick. (If you must cut one, see page 40.) Coat porous bricks with masonry sealer to minimize future repairs.

Chip out the damaged brick a piece at a time. Remove the old mortar, too, and thoroughly clean dust and debris from the cavity.

Dampen the surrounding bricks to retard evaporation, then lay fresh mortar on the cavity's bottom and sides.

Wet the new brick, slide it into place, and pack mortar into the joints. Scrape off any excess and scrub with a wet brush.

Match existing joints with the proper striking technique (see page 41 for the most common). Use a mason's strike or a piece of pipe.

BUILDING NEW WALLS

Admittedly, building a garden wall isn't the easiest around-the-house project you could tackle, but it's by no means impossible. If you've had a fair amount of do-it-yourself experience, the project should be well within your skills.

Dry walls (those without mortar) go up in a hurry because you're just piling layer upon layer of stone against the earth behind. *Wet walls* require more skill to build, as they use mortar for strength.

Before erecting a garden wall, plan its placement for maximum effect—visual and practical. And check to make sure that local codes don't restrict building in the location you've chosen.

DRY WALLS

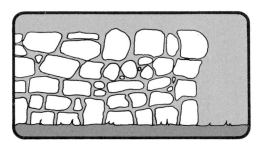

Rubble-stone walls go together like three-dimensional jigsaw puzzles. You simply stack them up against a bank of earth.

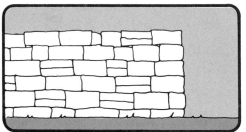

Ashlar stone is cut on four sides, so it's fairly easy to stack. You'll still have to do some final cutting and matching, though.

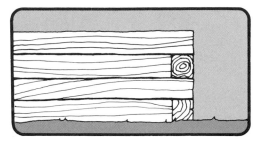

Railroad ties make terrific walls. Stack and nail them together, or anchor them in the ground with steel rods.

WET WALLS

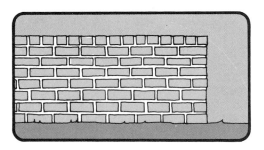

Brick walls, which require footings, gain their strength from mortar. (To learn about building them, see pages 40–43.)

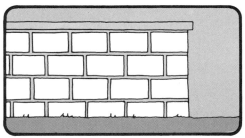

Like brick, mortared concrete block requires footings—but it goes up considerably faster. (See pages 38 and 39 for details.)

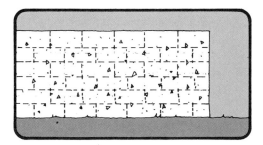

You can hurry your wall-building project along by dry-laying blocks then bonding them with fiberglass-reinforced mortar.

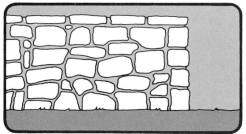

Field stone must be cut and fitted. You can use a heavier hand with the mortar than if you were working with brick or block.

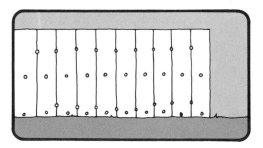

Poured concrete walls require forms, which you build or rent. These sturdy walls have footings and are reinforced with rods.

LAYING UP A DRY STONE WALL

Stacking stone is the oldest and easiest way to build a wall. Excellent for use in retaining walls, stone also makes nifty-looking decorative walls. A dry stone wall usually won't work as a screening wall, though, since you can't effectively stack the stones high enough to achieve the screening effect—four feet is usually considered tops.

Generally, you won't need to lay footings when erecting a dry stone wall. The wall will ride out frost heaves, and if damage does occur, you can repair it quickly.

If the wall will stand on its own and is for decorative purposes only, you should level the ground with a shovel before stacking the stone. This especially applies to ashlar stone (see opposite page). A fairly level base will let you lay it up like bricks.

If desired, you can "mortar" with earth, which makes the stone-fitting job easier. If you use earth, dampen the soil so it balls in your hand. But don't let it get too wet, as it's supposed to form a "pad" between the stone units.

If you're given the opportunity to pick and choose when you purchase stone for your wall, select medium to large stones instead of the smaller ones—they fill up space faster. For your smaller stone

requirements, break the stones with a mason's hammer. If you're stuck with a potpourri of sizes, use the larger stones as the base for the wall and lay the smaller ones atop.

Tools you'll need include a mason's hammer, brick chisel, shovel, small garden potting shovel, wooden stakes, and chalk line. If you plan on using earth mortar, you'll need a piece of hardboard or plywood to serve as a mixing surface and a hoe for blending the dirt and water to the proper consistency.

Lay out the wall, using stakes and a chalk line. Then dig a trench 6 to 12 inches deep and about 1 foot wider than the wall.

Fill the trench to within an inch of grade with pea gravel or small rocks. This base provides drainage and serves as a footing.

Begin the wall with stones that are large enough to span the gravel bed. Save the smaller ones for the top courses.

For the second and succeeding courses, make sure you stagger joints for greater strength. Tilt courses into the embankment.

For a tight cap, spread two inches of mortar along next-to-last course. Press in flat stones, filling gaps with small ones.

WORKING WITH MORTAR

Mortar is such a strong compound, some people may think it contains some mysterious ingredients that only masons can mix. Not so! It just contains cement, sand, and water, and anyone can mix it to perfection. For convenience, most people prefer to buy premixed mortar, even though it costs a bit more than purchasing the ingredients separately.

If you decide to mix your own, a good formula for retaining and screen walls is one part masonry cement to three parts sand. Use new masonry cement, and be sure the sand is clean.

You'll need a mortar box or the bed of a large wheelbarrow to mix the mortar, as well as a hoe to blend the cement, sand, and water.

Plan about four bags of masonry cement and 12 cubic feet of sand for a brick wall four inches thick and measuring 100 square feet in surface area. If that same wall is to be eight inches thick, buy eight bags of masonry cement and double the amount of sand. In estimating brick needs, figure seven bricks per square foot.

Store the unmixed cement in a dry place, and have the delivery truck dump the sand near the job site to save you time and effort in the mixing operation. Also keep the sand covered with plastic film at night and especially during any rain. The sand should ball in your hand without crumbling or leaking water, so make sure it's slightly damp before mixing it with the cement and water.

To mix mortar, combine the cement and the sand and blend it together with a hoe until its color is consistent throughout. Then add water, a little at a time, stirring the mixture with the hoe until it becomes smooth like thick mud. Test its consistency with a trowel as illustrated below. Mix small amounts of mortar at a time; it sets quickly and becomes useless after an hour or so—even faster in hot weather.

Using a Trowel

Practice makes perfect when it comes to working with mortar. So before attempting the finished project, build a test wall, then tear it down. You can reclaim the bricks or blocks, so your only "education expense"—and it's a minor one—is the mortar.

A trowel is used to place and trim mortar on bricks and blocks. It's also handy for making repairs in masonry walls (see pages 32 and 33). A lightweight trowel is the best for a beginning bricklayer. Buy a good one right from the start and it should last a lifetime.

Mix the mortar so it slumps slightly on the trowel. Slice off a section of "mud" and pick it up with a twist of your wrist.

Flick your wrist as you would flip a pancake, *"throwing"* the mortar in a smooth, lengthwise movement along the bricks or blocks.

Furrow the mortar, running your trowel down the center of the bricks. The procedure for blocks varies somewhat (see inset).

Press a dampened brick or a dry block firmly on the mortar. *Butter* one end of the next one and set it down (don't slide it).

Use the edge of your trowel to slice off mortar that oozes out. Use this excess to butter the next brick end.

Using a joint strike or piece of pipe, smooth mortar joints when they begin to stiffen (see pages 39 and 41).

CHOOSING OTHER MASONRY TOOLS

For brick and block walls, you'll need a long *mason's level*, *mason's hammer*, *cape chisel*, and *line blocks* (or nails) and *mason's line* to align the blocks or bricks in each course. Fabricate your own *hawk* and *mortar board* from ¾-inch exterior-grade plywood and pieces of 2x2. Additional tools handy to have include a *brick chisel, sledge,* and a *story pole* to align bricks or blocks as the courses are laid. Make the story pole with a straight 1x3 that's the same height as the wall.

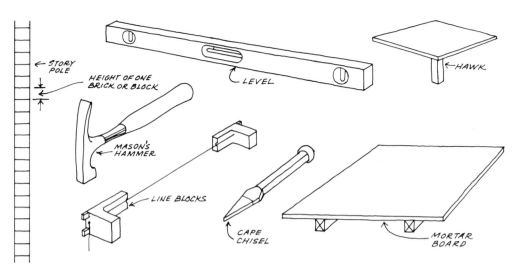

POURING FOOTINGS

Whether it's a brick, block, or stone wall you're constructing—except dry walls—you'll need to pour a footing. And as with all footings, those for walls should be below the frost line to avoid the ravages of cold weather. If you're unsure how deep the frost line is in your area, check with your community's building department or a local contractor.

Since footings usually require lots of concrete, it's best to buy premixed material and have it trucked in. This will save you time and plenty of back-breaking work.

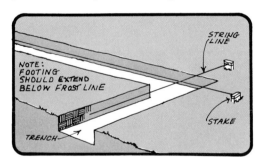

Stake out lines for the wall, then dig a trench twice the width of the footing. First courses will be below grade level.

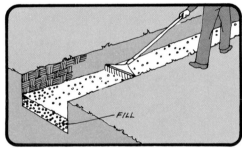

Place six inches of rock or gravel in the trench for drainage. Then level the material by pulling a garden rake across the top of it.

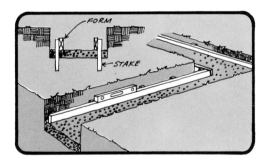

Stake the forms securely, making sure that they are perfectly level and square. Drive stakes on the outside of the forms.

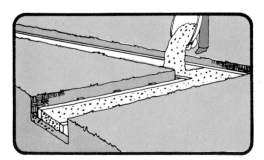

Coat sides of forms with old motor oil for easy removal later. Pour concrete, and jab with a shovel to compact it.

Strike off excess concrete, seesawing a 2x4 screed along top edges of forms. Have a friend shovel away the excess.

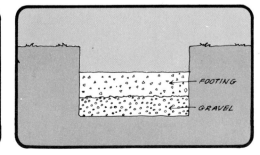

If ground is hard, you can place concrete without forms. Dig a straight-sided trench the width of the footing, as shown.

WORKING WITH CONCRETE BLOCK

Mustering the strength to maneuver the blocks into position is the main difficulty you'll have in laying up a block wall. Even the lighter-weight aggregate blocks aren't exactly light, especially after you've lifted a few.

As when building brick walls, use a mortar mix consisting of one part cement to three parts sand. Don't use as much water, though, or the heavy blocks will compact the mixture. Mix small batches of mortar at a time; it sets quickly.

Lay out your block wall in multiples of eight inches. This will save you plenty of work cutting the units to fit. (Standard blocks measure 8x8x16 inches including the joints. Determine the number of blocks you need from this standard measurement.) The sketch below shows various types of blocks along with their actual sizes. Some blocks are sized to accommodate a ½-inch mortar joint.

Block walls need footings, which should be below the frost line. Ask a contractor how deep the frost line is in your area. For information on how to pour footings, see the previous page.

To some people, concrete blocks aren't as aesthetically pleasing as bricks, stone, lumber, and other materials. Solve this problem by using decorative screen blocks, which are manufactured in a variety of patterns and some special shapes. You can paint the blocks with masonry-type finishes, if desired.

Unlike bricks, which must be dampened with water before they're laid, concrete blocks should be bone-dry as they're mortared and set. Keep them under cover before you use them.

Tools you'll need for working with concrete blocks include a trowel, mason's hammer, brick chisel, joint strike, level, carpenter's square, line blocks and mason's line, and a story pole.

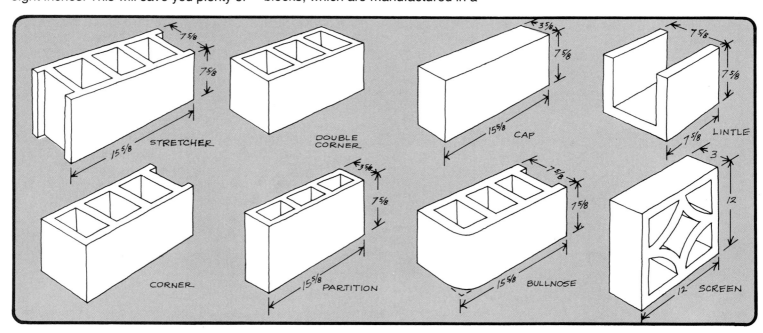

Cutting Concrete Blocks

Mark a line around the perimeter of block. Then, with a chisel and hammer, tap along line. The block will crack at the line.

Reinforcing Block Walls

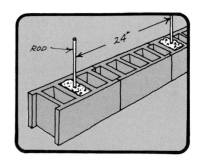

For walls higher than four feet, sink metal reinforcing rods into the wet footing. Slip block over rods and fill cores with concrete.

LAYING A BLOCK WALL

"Start even and square; finish even and square" is an old adage that's especially true when you lay blocks or bricks; the units must be level, plumb, and square. If you're off an inch or so at the start, the error compounds itself as each block is set into position. You also must remember to keep the mortar joints consistent in width, or the blocks won't align properly along courses.

Set the ends and corners first—never begin in the center of the wall. And double-check all measurements to make sure the first blocks are level and square.

Next, to ensure that you lay the blocks level and plumb, stretch a mason's line between line blocks (or nails) at either end of the wall. Move the line blocks up after each course is completed. Don't rely on the line blocks alone, though. Use a story pole to guide you (see page 37), and check each three-block section with a level as you go. If you spot an error, remove the guilty blocks immediately and start again.

Before mixing mortar, lay blocks along footing to check fit. Use plywood strips for joint spacing. Mark spacings on footing.

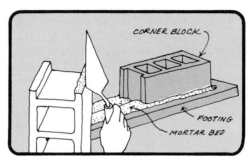

Throw down 2-inch-deep lines of mortar and set end block. Butter and set second block. Smaller holes in blocks face down.

Set three blocks, then check for level and plumb. Make minor adjustments by tapping blocks with trowel handle. Reset if needed.

Build corners or ends when first course is laid. Check again with level and story pole. If they're off, pull blocks and start again.

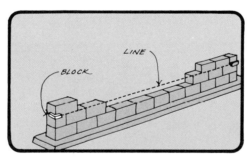

When corners or ends are three or four courses high, stretch a line between them. Mason's line blocks (or nails) hold it taut.

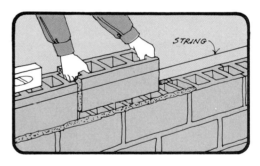

Lay blocks between corners, using the line for a level. Lift blocks into position; don't slide them—you'll foul the mortar.

Butter both ends of last block in each course and ends of blocks that fit against last block. Carefully slip block into position.

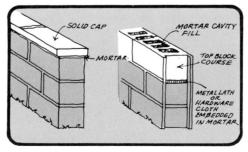

Use solid caps to close the wall. Or, sandwich mesh in last mortar joint and then fill the cores in the top block with mortar.

Use a joint strike or a pipe to smooth mortar. Finish job by wiping joints with burlap; remove mortar from block faces.

WORKING WITH BRICK

Laying up a brick wall is one of those projects that's more time-consuming than difficult. The reason: for every square foot of wall, you'll need to place approximately seven bricks. So, even a short wall translates into much work.

Many of the tools and techniques that are used for raising block walls work equally well for brick walls. So before you undertake your project, refer to pages 36 and 37 for information on tools you'll need, pouring footings, estimating material needs, and working with mortar.

When shopping for bricks, you have three options: *SW (severe-weathering) brick,* used mainly in cold climates; *MW (moderate-weathering) brick,* for areas with moderate temperatures year-round; and *NW (no-weathering) brick,* for use in mild climates and interior construction such as fireplaces. For exterior retaining walls, purchase SW brick, since it withstands frost better below grade.

You also can choose between standard-size bricks or jumbo or irregular sizes. This is pretty much a matter of personal preference.

For strength, brick screen and retaining walls should be of two-tier rather than one-tier construction. This will

double the number of bricks you need for the project, so figure it in your estimates when you lay out the wall. You'll also have to order more cement and sand for the mortar. To be on the safe side, overestimate your needs so that you won't be caught short of material.

Plan a route for the delivery truck, bearing in mind that your driveway may not withstand the load. For small quantities, you may be better off to wheelbarrow the bricks from the curb to the site where you'll be building. Store bricks up off the ground on a wooden platform, and cover them with polyethylene so they don't absorb water.

Fitting Bricks Together

Although bricks are all rectangular in shape, you can fit and lay them in a surprising number of ways that not only add strength to the wall but also give it a

distinct character of its own. On the facing page are some of the more popular bonds.

To get the design you want, you'll have to cut some of the bricks to fit. The tools needed to do this include a marking pencil, hammer, and brick chisel. First

mark all four sides of the brick where you want to cut it. Then score the brick along the line with a brick chisel, tapping the chisel gently with a hammer. The brick should break cleanly at this point.

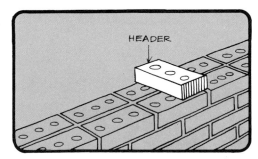

Stretchers, laid flat and with face outward, are an integral part of every brick wall, regardless of the bond you choose.

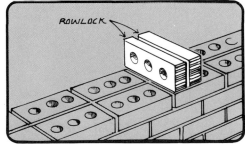

Headers laid every few courses (or at the top of a wall) add strength. Headers run at right angles to stretchers.

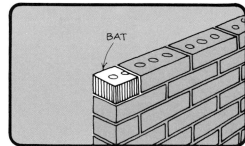

Bats are half-bricks. Use them on ends of walls and as closure units for header courses. Split full bricks to make bats.

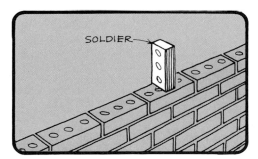

Set bricks on their ends, face outward, and you have *soldiers.* Soldiers add design variation but little strength.

Rowlock headers are set across stretchers, but with their edges up. Rowlocks are quite often used to cap-off a wall.

Choosing a Bond

The pattern in which you set your bricks is called a "bond." As the bricks are laid, they're staggered so that vertical joints are never in alignment (except for a stacked bond). Staggered joints give the wall lots of additional strength.

You also can give more strength to two-tiered walls by using metal wall ties between the tiers. The ties, which are positioned at various intervals along the wall, lay across the bricks.

Before you make a decision on the type of wall bond you want, it's a good idea to buy a hundred or so bricks and build a test wall without mortar. Try several different bonds, *then* make your commitment.

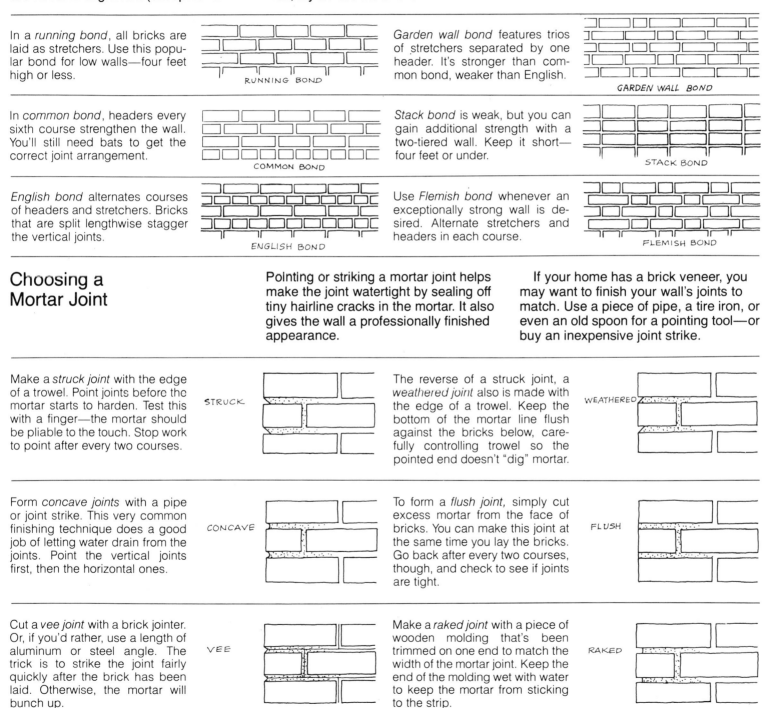

In a *running bond*, all bricks are laid as stretchers. Use this popular bond for low walls—four feet high or less.

RUNNING BOND

Garden wall bond features trios of stretchers separated by one header. It's stronger than common bond, weaker than English.

GARDEN WALL BOND

In *common bond*, headers every sixth course strengthen the wall. You'll still need bats to get the correct joint arrangement.

COMMON BOND

Stack bond is weak, but you can gain additional strength with a two-tiered wall. Keep it short—four feet or under.

STACK BOND

English bond alternates courses of headers and stretchers. Bricks that are split lengthwise stagger the vertical joints.

ENGLISH BOND

Use *Flemish bond* whenever an exceptionally strong wall is desired. Alternate stretchers and headers in each course.

FLEMISH BOND

Choosing a Mortar Joint

Pointing or striking a mortar joint helps make the joint watertight by sealing off tiny hairline cracks in the mortar. It also gives the wall a professionally finished appearance.

If your home has a brick veneer, you may want to finish your wall's joints to match. Use a piece of pipe, a tire iron, or even an old spoon for a pointing tool—or buy an inexpensive joint strike.

Make a *struck joint* with the edge of a trowel. Point joints before the mortar starts to harden. Test this with a finger—the mortar should be pliable to the touch. Stop work to point after every two courses.

STRUCK

The reverse of a struck joint, a *weathered joint* also is made with the edge of a trowel. Keep the bottom of the mortar line flush against the bricks below, carefully controlling trowel so the pointed end doesn't "dig" mortar.

WEATHERED

Form *concave joints* with a pipe or joint strike. This very common finishing technique does a good job of letting water drain from the joints. Point the vertical joints first, then the horizontal ones.

CONCAVE

To form a *flush joint,* simply cut excess mortar from the face of bricks. You can make this joint at the same time you lay the bricks. Go back after every two courses, though, and check to see if joints are tight.

FLUSH

Cut a *vee joint* with a brick jointer. Or, if you'd rather, use a length of aluminum or steel angle. The trick is to strike the joint fairly quickly after the brick has been laid. Otherwise, the mortar will bunch up.

VEE

Make a *raked joint* with a piece of wooden molding that's been trimmed on one end to match the width of the mortar joint. Keep the end of the molding wet with water to keep the mortar from sticking to the strip.

RAKED

LAYING A BRICK WALL

As with concrete block walls, you should begin building brick walls from the ends or corners, then fill in to the middle of the wall.

String loose bricks along the length of the footings so they're in easy reach as you build the wall. The bricks should be wet when laid; sprinkle them with a hose before you start and keep them wet in a bucket as you work. If at all possible, have a friend mix the mortar for you as you lay the bricks. This will speed the job and keep the mortar fresh as well.

The *starter* or first *course* of brick must be absolutely level and square on the footing. If it's not, remove the bricks from the footing, clean away the mortar on both the footing and the bricks, and start again.

Continue with the next brick units and courses, double- and triple-checking each one with a level, square, and story pole (see pages 37 and 39).

Building Up Corners

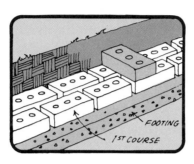

Dry-lay the first course, spacing each exactly ½ inch apart. Check spacing between tiers by laying a brick across them.

Soak the bricks thoroughly before laying them. Dry bricks absorb water from the mortar and as a result weaken the wall.

Start at an end or corner. Pick up three or four dry-laid bricks, and throw and furrow mortar line. Then lay the bricks; check level.

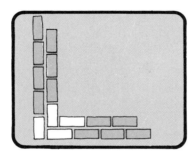

Positioning at the corners is crucial, so check your arrangement carefully. Note that joints between bricks are staggered.

Check bricks carefully for alignment, as well as level and plumb. If a brick is slightly out, tap it gently into place.

Build up corners, ends, and a section every 10 feet in long walls. Use a story pole to check for alignment with the rest of the wall.

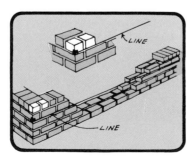

To ensure that all bricks in each course are correctly positioned, use a length of mason's line stretched between line blocks.

Lay headers every sixth course on common-bond walls. But first trowel mortar between the tiers—this makes for a stronger wall.

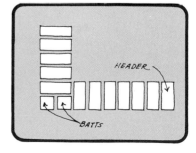

Turn headers around corners as illustrated. You'll have to cut a few bats from full bricks to form the proper corner bond.

42

Completing the Courses

Align intervening bricks with string line, raising it after each course. If a brick is out of line, remove it and start again.

To lay a closure brick, butter mortar on both ends and on ends of bricks in place. Gently place it between the other bricks.

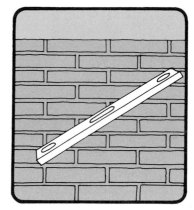

A level makes an excellent straightedge. Check your work by holding it diagonally as well as horizontally and vertically.

Strike joints after every few courses—verticals first, then horizontals. (For different striking techniques, see page 41.)

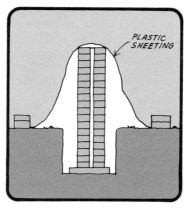

When you finish for the day, scrub the bricks to remove loose mortar. Then wet down the wall and cover it with polyethylene.

After three weeks or so, scrub the bricks with a mild solution of muriatic acid. This removes any mortar that remains on them.

Capping Off a Brick Wall

When it's possible, top a wall with *coping*—bricks, stone, tiles, or precast concrete—to keep the water away from the bricks below. The coping should slope just enough to shed water, and if possible, project about ½ inch from the face of the wall so water won't run down the wall.

You can pitch the cap by building the mortar bed higher on one side of the wall. To add more strength to the entire unit, stagger coping joints with the vertical joints in the wall.

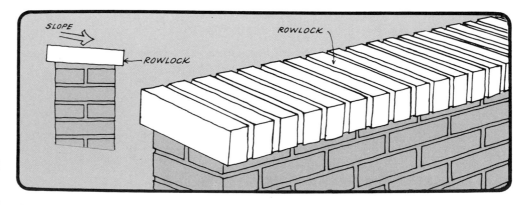

A course of rowlocks is the simplest way to top a wall. Choose bricks at least one inch longer than wall width.

WALKS AND STEPS

Paving encompasses everything from a series of stepping-stones to an interstate highway. Materials commonly used include concrete, brick, stone, asphalt, and even wood and gravel.

This chapter covers only those aspects of home paving not treated elsewhere in the book. For more about laying concrete surfaces, see pages 5 and 10–16; to learn about setting bricks or stones in sand, see page 9.

Paving of any type depends on proper drainage to protect it against damage from freezing and thawing. Underneath, a porous base—usually sand or gravel—drains away water before it can do any harm to the surface.

Ignore a paving problem and it will only get worse. The repairs that are shown below and on the next page call for only a modest expenditure of time and money.

Laying new paving materials is a bigger job, of course, but you can easily master the basics (see pages 46–47). And since even a large paving project usually can be broken down into a series of smaller ones, the work needn't be overwhelming.

SOLVING PAVING PROBLEMS

Frost, settlement, de-icing compounds, and tree roots all take their toll on even the best-laid paving. Fortunately, all you need for most repairs is a few dollars' worth of patching materials and simple hand tools.

Before you attack a problem, though, first find out what caused it. In chronic situations—usually the result of an inadequate base—you may be better off to rip up the old paving and start over.

LEVELING WALKS

To even-up a heaved or sunken walk, pry up the out-of-keel piece and add to or remove what's underneath. Flagstones, bricks, and small pieces of concrete lift out with little persuasion. Bigger slabs may demand a pick, wrecking bar, or pipe. Chop away any roots you encounter with a hatchet or ax.

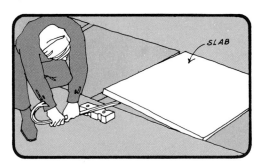

Work a pick or wrecking bar under the settled section, lift it high enough to get underneath, then prop it up with a 2x4.

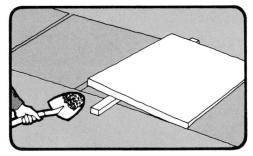

Fill underneath with equal parts sand, sifted dirt, and cement. Tamp, if possible, or overfill to allow for settling.

If a heaved or sunken section is too large to lift, score near center and break slab with a chisel and hammer. Wear goggles.

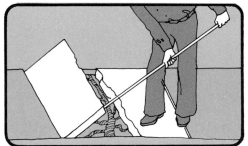

When a piece breaks free, pry and block it up, then chop out roots or add fill. If section is high, remove dirt.

Level the section, then cement the pieces together. Or, fill the crack with asphalt. Put sand on asphalt to prevent tracking.

44

REPAIRING DAMAGED STEPS

Cracked, chipped, sunken, or heaved steps pose a serious safety hazard—and if you neglect repairs, you could end up having to replace the entire structure someday. Clearly, it pays to keep an eye out for problems and attend to them right away.

Steps differ considerably. Some have a brick superstructure and concrete treads. Others are all brick; still others are solid concrete.

With brick-and-concrete construction, you have to guard against moisture getting in the bricks' mortar joints.

Point any crumbling materials as shown on page 32. Patch the treads as you would any concrete surface (see below and page 5).

If your steps are constructed entirely of brick, look for mortar damage in the treads, where the treads meet the risers, and in joints between the steps and house or walk. Again, point if this is necessary.

To replace a broken brick, chisel out the mortar around it, chop out the pieces, and replace (see page 33). If you need more room to maneuver, remove and replace bricks on either side of the broken one, too.

Repair all-concrete steps as illustrated below. Note that it's important to

"undercut" old concrete so that the patch can get a secure hold. Use a cold chisel or brick chisel for this operation, then thoroughly flush away debris with a hose. Keep the crack damp until you fill it.

For patching material, mix one part cement with three parts sand and just enough water to make it doughy. Or purchase one of the special premixed patching compounds available in cartridges. Trowel this mixture into the damaged area, packing with the trowel's tip and smoothing with its edge.

To repair chips, spalled sections, and other damage that can't be undercut, use special epoxy patching cement mixed with sand according to the manufacturer's specifications.

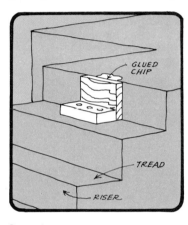

Sometimes, you can glue pieces back in place with epoxy cement. Clean area, press piece in place, and "clamp" as shown.

Epoxy cement revives spalled surfaces, too. Break away loose concrete, then trowel on mix, feathering edges.

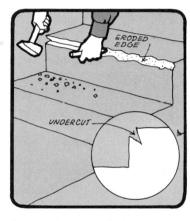

If an entire edge is broken, cut concrete back to make a V-groove. Groove helps hold the patch in place. Clean the area.

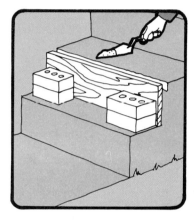

Press a board against the edge of the patch to serve as a form. Apply concrete, packing the groove full. Level top of patch.

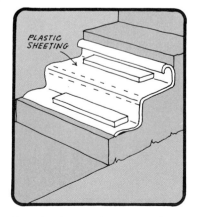

To make the patch stronger, keep damp for about a week. Cover the repair with polyethylene and weight it down with scrap lumber.

Level a settled stoop as you would a slab (opposite). You may need a helper for the job and maybe a second wrecking bar.

Fill joint between foundation and stoop or steps with concrete joint filler, latex caulk, oakum, or an asphalt expansion strip.

LAYING NEW PAVING MATERIALS

Garden paving offers an excellent opportunity for you to learn about the basics of working with masonry. Unlike the bigger jobs of constructing a patio (see pages 8–16), you needn't move a lot of earth, prepare extensive footings and forms, or master any special techniques.

Certain projects go faster than others, of course. For a rustic pathway that rises and falls with the terrain, you need to excavate only a few inches, pour a loose-fill base of sand or gravel, then lay one or a combination of the materials shown below. On land that's high and drains reasonably well, you may not even need a base for the paving.

For the more formal look of an arrow-straight walk, you'll probably need a concrete base, but it needn't be more than 4 inches thick, and doesn't require reinforcement.

If you have a lot of paving to do, use materials that you can fabricate yourself or buy at home improvement centers. This way, you can do a few sections at a time, without a weekend-after-weekend work hangover.

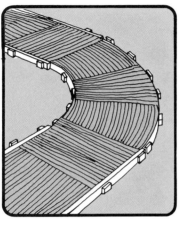

If soil drains well, concrete walks can be as thin as 3 inches. Make forms from 1x4s and shape curves with ¼-inch tempered hardboard. Broom-finish surface.

To cast your own stepping-stones, first build a form on a level spot. Then add a layer of sand and 2 inches of concrete. Screed the units with a 2x4.

Asphalt makes an economical paving material, but it needs a firm base of rock or tamped sand on which to lie. You can color asphalt with special paints.

Retain loose-fill materials with wood, brick, or block edging. Build forms as you would for a patio (see page 11). Use various gravels for interest.

Brick—a paving classic—works well with formal or informal settings. Set paving bricks on a mortar base, or on sand as you would a patio (see page 9).

Flagstones may be set on sand or in mortar. Use 2-inch minimum thickness over sand; ½ to 1 inch on concrete. Choose modular rectangles or irregular shapes.

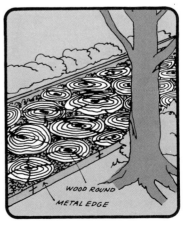

Wood blocks or rounds, made by slicing timbers or logs, give a rustic character to walks. Use redwood, cypress, cedar, or a rot-treated wood. Set in sand.

BUILDING STEPS

Well-constructed in-ground steps not only get you from one level to another, they also hold back erosion. Plan them as you would a retaining wall (see pages 31 and 35). Notch steps into slopes wherever possible; otherwise, they may begin to slide in a season or two.

Select materials to match or contrast with the pathways at either end. The drawings below show six popular options and there are dozens of other possibilities. Just be sure to firmly anchor whichever material you choose and provide adequate drainage. It's best to pitch *treads* (the parts you walk on) slightly downhill or to one side so water will run off.

Once you have made a decision on materials, you'll need to answer some questions. How many steps will you need to get from one level to another? How deep should you make each tread? How high should each vertical *riser* be?

Begin by measuring the vertical distance, *rise*, from the bottom to top level. To do this, first drive a tall stake at the bottom and stretch a line from the stake to the top. Level this line, then measure from the point where it joins the stake to the ground below. Double-check this measurement. If it's off even an inch or two, you could end up with unequally spaced risers—a sure way to cause people accidents.

Next, determine the approximate height you'd like the risers to be. This can vary from 3 to 9 inches. Low risers—usually with deep treads—provide a leisurely transition from one level to another; plan shallow treads and higher risers for service areas where you'll want to get from one level to another more rapidly.

Now, to determine the total *run*, measure the length of the line you've stretched from the stake to the top of the slope. By juggling this dimension and the height of the risers, you can compute both the number of steps you'll need and the distance each tread will measure from front to rear (more about this on page 20).

Make treads a minimum of 10 inches deep (12 to 15 inches is a more comfortable depth), but for a graceful, terraced effect, treads can be 3 feet deep or more.

Excavate carefully, using a spade to keep the cuts' sides straight. In calculating how deep to dig, be sure to include a couple of inches for a sand or gravel base—and don't forget to allow for the thickness of the treads in planning the height of each riser, especially at the top and bottom.

If you can't notch-in your steps, you'll have to build them up—a big job with most materials. If you choose masonry, be certain to pour footings first. Or construct a wood, open-riser staircase, as shown on page 20.

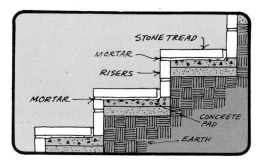

Railroad ties make excellent risers. The treads shown here are gravel, but you could also use brick, block, or concrete.

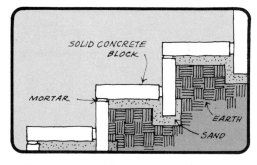

Solid concrete blocks offer a quick way to build steps. Sink them into a sand base. Be sure to pitch slightly for drainage.

To construct brick steps, first lay down a bed of sand, set concrete slabs atop, then set the bricks in mortar, as shown.

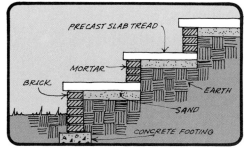

Flagstones rest on brick, wood, or broken stone risers. Set them on sand/concrete pads in mortar for the best stability.

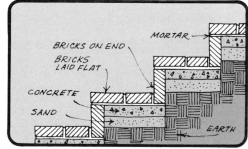

Precast slabs are usually heavy enough to hold themselves in position—but it's wise to put them on a firm base for stability.

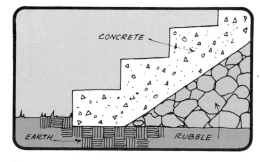

Cast concrete steps take lots of form-building and material. To save concrete, dump clean stones or bricks into form first.

INDEX

Have BETTER HOMES AND
GARDENS® magazine delivered to
your door. For information, write to:
MR. ROBERT AUSTIN
P.O. BOX 4536
DES MOINES, IA 50336